SEVEN WEEKS

OF

GROWING UP

TO THE

HEAD

Your Personal Discipleship Journey and Journal

by

George O. McCalep, Jr., Ph.D.

Orman Press
Lithonia, Georgia

Seven Weeks of Growing Up to the Head
Your Personal Discipleship Journey and Journal

by
George O. McCalep, Jr., Ph.D.

Copyright © 2004
Orman Press, Inc.

ISBN: 1-891773-55-0

Scripture quotations are taken from THE HOLY BIBLE, *King James Version*. Bible quotations marked NIV are from the Holy Bible, New International Version, copyright © 1973, 1978, 1984 Zondervan Publishing House.

Printed in the United States of America

10 9 8 7 6 5 4 3 2 1

Orman Press, Inc.
Lithonia, Georgia

Table of Contents

About This Study i

    What is Growing Up to the Head?
    Why Seven Weeks?
    Purpose
    Using This Book

Introduction v

    Why Grow Up to the Head?
    Call for Commitment
    Objectives

Week 1: Growing Up in Everlasting Joy 1

Week 2: Growing Up in His Grace and Reconciliation 33

Week 3: Growing Up in His Purpose and Prayer 61

Week 4: Growing Up in His Love and Likeness 91

Week 5: Growing Up in His Spirit 119

Week 6: Growing Up in Relationships 147

Week 7: Growing Up in His Strength 173

End of the Journey: Beginning of Discipleship 197

About This Study

What is Growing Up to the Head?

The title of this study is based on the truth found in the book of Ephesians, where God symbolizes us, the body of Christ, as having individual parts or members. Christ is the Head and the church is the body. The Head is perfect, but the body is imperfect. Therefore, the body should grow up to the Head.

Why Seven Weeks?

First, I learned that seven is a perfect number in the Hebrew language. Secondly, I learned in behavioral science, any principles of practice that exceed seven are counter-productive; therefore, my first book entitled *Faithful Over a Few Things* dealt with seven critical church growth principles, and yes, there are seven days in a week. Thus, we have *Seven Weeks of Growing Up to the Head*.

Purpose

This book is designed to guide you in growing up to the Head, our Lord and Savior, Jesus Christ, in seven weeks. *Seven Weeks of Growing Up to the Head* is about individual spiritual growth based on the book of Ephesians. The aim is to grow the church numerically through individual spiritual growth. Through this daily study, church members, leaders and pastors can participate in the ministry of church growth.

Using This Book

Seven Weeks of Growing Up to the Head is based on the premise that individual spiritual growth leads to collective church growth. This book contains a course introduction and seven weeks of daily study. Each daily study includes:

- **Acknowledging God** – This daily opening and closing prayer is located at the beginning of each of the seven weeks. The purpose of the prayer is to acknowledge God and what He has done or is about to do in your life during each daily study. Remember to pray each prayer before and at the end of each day's study. Expect God to establish this principle in your head and heart.

- **Spiritual Truth** – This personalized truth is the focus of each daily lesson and is designed to penetrate your heart.

- **Memory Verse** – This is the Scripture that we will focus on all week. Read the verse and think about its meaning. Say the verse aloud. Memorize the verse in parts over the first three days. By the fourth day, you should be able to put the entire verse together. Continue repeating the entire verse from memory for the next three days. By day seven, you should have the Scripture hidden in your heart.

- **Reading References** – These Scripture readings support the day's study.

- **Additional Reading References** – These are additional readings that are too long to print here. Therefore, it is necessary to use your Bible when doing this study.

- **Journal It: Continuing the Growth** – The daily journal pages provide thought provoking questions to reinforce the lesson and lead you in applying God's Word. In order to grow spiritually, it is critical to record your thoughts and God's responses.

- **Reflections** – Use these pages to record the spiritual truths that God has revealed to you throughout the week.

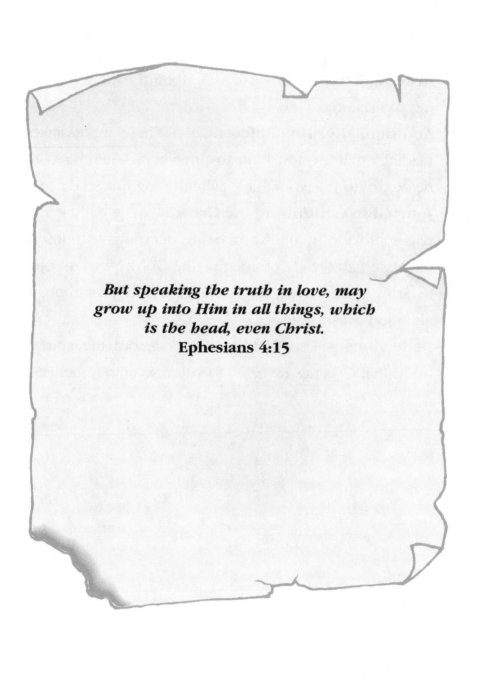

But speaking the truth in love, may grow up into Him in all things, which is the head, even Christ.

Ephesians 4:15

Introduction

A Call for Collective Numerical Growth Through Individual Spiritual Growth in the Body of Christ

*S*even Weeks of Growing Up to the Head is a call for Christians to fulfill their duty to grow—spiritually and numerically. God wants us to make disciples, not just Christians. A disciple is a disciplined follower of Christ who is willing to make another. We need to be about the business of preparing the "bride," the church, for the "bridegroom," Christ.

Seven Weeks of Growing Up to the Head means becoming spiritually mature by growing into the fullness of Christ so we can do the things that the Head is directing us to do.

In Colossians 1:18, Paul writes that Christ is the Head of the church, which is His body. There is nothing wrong with the Head. The Head is perfect.

The church is the fullness of God. It is the body, which is made up of baptized believers. We are the church and God is calling us, the body of Christ, to be filled up to the

Head. God is calling His church to grow up. Believers, both individually and collectively, are to grow up in His fullness. The problem with growing up to the Head is:

- **Conflict and incompleteness.** The same conflict and sense of incompleteness that dwells in a person who has not grown up to the Head can be present in the church.

- **The body does not match the Head.** The Head constantly sends messages to the body through His Word and His Spirit, but the body cannot do what the Head says because it is too weak and sickly.

- **Not joining God's purpose.** God in Christ is purposeful and intentional and, unless believers join God's purpose and intention, they will remain immature children.

- **Sickly leadership.** If the church's leadership is sickly, the church will simply limp along, never growing to its full potential. If the individual members are spiritually anemic, then the church body can do no better. A sickly church body will always lag pitifully behind the Head.

Why Grow Up to the Head?

Seven Weeks of Growing Up to the Head is based on the assumption that individual spiritual growth is a precursor to meaningful numerical church growth. It is possible to have church growth without spiritual growth because many people desire to be entertained; however, spiritual growth yields much deeper levels of church growth.

Growing up to the Head and growing the church is the role and responsibility of every Christian. Specific reasons for growing up to the Head are:

- **Numerical growth of the church.** God's kingdom cannot grow unless the members of the church grow. This includes your local church. Many churches are not growing numerically because their members are not growing spiritually.

- **Jesus desires a full house.** A filled people produce a full house. Fill the people, and they will fill the house. A full house on Sunday morning can be the result of members growing up in the fullness of Christ.

- **To make disciples who will make more disciples (Matthew 28:16–20 TLB).** The word *make* is the only word of command in the Great Commission. The Greek text is interpreted, "as you are going, make disciples." The instruction is clear, "make disciples." People cannot *go* because they have not been *made* disciples. Make disciples, and they will go because evangelism is not an option for mature Christians.

- **So the church (the body of Christ) can carry out the ministry God has called it to do (Ephesians 4:12).** This is a paradigm shift. Traditionally, people expect the pastor to do ministry, but God has called all Christians to the work of ministry.

- **So that believers, both individually and collectively, will grow into the fullness of Christ and be all that He has called us to be.**

Call for Commitment

I recommend that you complete this study with a partner. The intimacy of a partner affords the transparency that is needed for the transformational changes we, as Christians, are being called to make within the body of Christ. Having a partner will also help you take a closer, deeper look at how you contribute to the building up or tearing down of God's kingdom. Allow time to process the content and share growth experiences so that the study moves beyond information and inspiration, and results in spiritual transformation.

God is calling all Christian believers to build His kingdom by becoming disciples and making others. Below is space for you and your partner to commit.

Will you answer the call?

Yes! I commit to this seven week study of growing up to the Head and into the fullness of Christ.

John H. Davis '74   _2/27/2005_
_____   _____
         Signature   Date

Yes! I commit to this seven week study of growing up to the Head and into the fullness of Christ.

_____   _____
         Signature   Date

Objectives

Now that you are fully committed to *Seven Weeks of Growing Up to the Head,* the question is: How do I grow up to the Head? The book of Ephesians and *Seven Weeks of Growing Up to the Head* will help you. The goal of this study is collective numerical church growth through individual spiritual growth. In other words, the goal is for you and your partner to grow spiritually so that the church will grow numerically.

Maturing spiritually means that you will grow to live in the fullness of Christ and that you will:

- have His everlasting joy within you.
- recognize God's grace in your life.
- reconcile all broken relationships and be in a right relationship with God.
- know your purpose in His kingdom.
- pray the way God wants you to pray.
- know the love of Christ.
- become like Christ, righteous and holy.
- be filled with the Holy Spirit.
- submit all your relationships unto God.
- rely on God's strength for everything.
- make other disciples.

Opening Prayer

It is important that you begin this spiritual journey with prayer. Read the following prayer aloud to invite the Holy Spirit into your study and surrender all to Him.

Acknowledging God

*Dear Lord, my Father in Heaven, I praise You as the Head of the church and my life. Now Holy Spirit, dwell with me as I go on this journey of **Seven Weeks of Growing Up to the Head**. As I go through this journey, speak to my heart. Open the ears and eyes of my heart to understand and accept Your calling for me to grow into Your fullness. As I go through this journey, I pray that Your everlasting joy will flow within me. Help me to appreciate more and more, Your grace in my life. Help me to reconcile all broken relationships in my life so that I will be in a right relationship with You. Impassion me to know my purpose in Your kingdom and to pray the way You want me to. More than anything, help me to know Your love so that I can become more like You, Christ Jesus, Holy and righteous, and filled with Your Holy Spirit. Teach me how to submit all my relationships unto You, especially the one I have with You. Help me to rely on Your strength for everything. All this I ask so that I may become a disciple that will make other disciples. In Your Name, Lord Jesus, I give You thanks. Amen!*

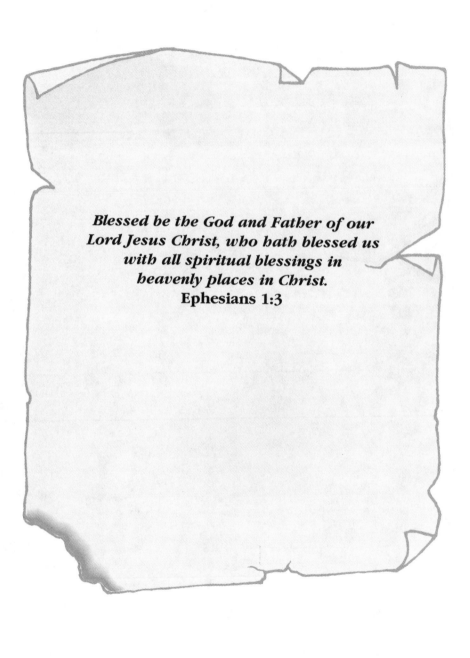

*Blessed be the God and Father of our
Lord Jesus Christ, who hath blessed us
with all spiritual blessings in
heavenly places in Christ.*
Ephesians 1:3

Growing Up to the Head in...
Everlasting Joy

Acknowledging God

Dear God, today I acknowledge you as the giver of everlasting joy. I am joyful that you have chosen me to be a member of your family. Help me to grow out of materialism and into Your fullness. Teach me to focus on the things that please You. Forgive me for failing to see the true value of the spiritual blessings You have given to bring me joy. Teach me how to grow up to the Head in Your everlasting joy. In Your Name, Lord Jesus, I give You thanks. Amen!

Week 1 ◆ Day 1

Spiritual Truth:

Everlasting joy comes through knowing God.

Memory Verse:

"Blessed be the God and Father of our Lord Jesus Christ, who hath blessed us with all spiritual blessings in heavenly places in Christ" (Ephesians 1:3).

Reading References:

"Make me to hear joy and gladness; that the bones which thou hast broken may rejoice... Restore unto me the joy of thy salvation; and uphold me with thy free spirit" (Psalm 51:8, 12).

"The glory of the Lord shall endure for ever: the Lord shall rejoice in his works" (Psalm 104:31).

"These things have I spoken unto you, that my joy might remain in you, and that your joy might be full" (John 15:11).

"But the fruit of the Spirit is love, joy, peace, longsuffering, gentleness, goodness, faith" (Galatians 5:22).

What is "Everlasting Joy?"

The *Holman Bible Dictionary*[1] defines *joy* as:

> The happy state that results from knowing and serving God...The fruit of a right relationship with God. It is not something people can create by their own efforts...Joy in the Christian life is in direct proportion as believers walk with the Lord.

In Ephesians 1:3, the apostle Paul revealed his excitement about God's worthiness and what God had already done. What had God done? God had blessed believers with spiritual blessings. We too must become excited about what God has already done, if we are going to be His instruments.

Paul understood what it meant to grow up in everlasting joy. This was a man who sang songs of praise while in jail. Paul got "caught up" in his praise.

A believer who has grown up in the joy that only comes from God can easily get "caught up" in praise. Maybe you have been in the midst of a difficult situation—death, financial ruin or trouble with your child. When you have grown up in everlasting joy, you are still able to praise God, even in the midst of living hell.

---

1. *Holman Bible Dictionary*, Trent C. Butler, ed. (Nashville: Holman Bible Publishers, 1991), s.v. "Joy."

Journal It: Continuing the Growth

God knows joy (Psalms 104:31) and He wants us to have it. Joy is a fruit of the Spirit (Galatians 5:22); therefore, all believers should have it. Joy in the Lord enables us to enjoy all that God has given us. John 15:11 makes it clear that God desires that we not only have joy, but that our joy be full. The Greek translation of *full* is "complete, perfect, filled up." However, according to Psalm 51:8 and 12, sin robs us of our joy. Is there any sin in your life that is robbing you of God's everlasting joy? If so, what are you willing to do to rid your life of this sin so you can experience God's everlasting joy in its fullness?

Yes.

_____

_____

_____

_____

_____

_____

_____

_____

_____

_____

_____

_____

_____

_____

_____

_____

Journal It: Continuing the Growth

Week 1 ◆ Day 2

Spiritual Truth:

All material possessions are temporary.

Memory Verse:

"Blessed be the God and Father of our Lord Jesus Christ, who hath blessed us with all spiritual blessings in heavenly places in Christ" (Ephesians 1:3).

Reading References:

"Lay not up for yourselves treasures upon earth, where moth and rust doth corrupt, and where thieves break through and steal: But lay up for yourselves treasures in heaven, where neither moth nor rust doth corrupt, and where thieves do not break through nor steal: For where your treasure is, there will your heart be also" (Matthew 6:19–21).

"And that which fell among thorns are they, which, when they have heard, go forth, and are choked with cares and riches and pleasures of this life, and bring no fruit to perfection" (Luke 8:14).

Additional Reading References:

Ecclesiastes 2:1–11

How Do We Grow Up in Everlasting Joy? (Part I)

Growing up to the Head in His everlasting joy means placing greater value on spiritual blessings than anything else. One way of doing this is by growing out of materialism.

Materialism is placing an unhealthy value on things, especially money. In order to grow up to the Head in His everlasting joy, we must grow out of materialism (See Ecclesiastes 2:1–11, Matthew 6:19–21 and Luke 8:14).

Growing up in His everlasting joy means realizing and appreciating our spiritual blessings, which are superior to material blessings. The unrighteous may receive material blessings, but God provides spiritual blessings only to those who are in Christ.

Growing up in His everlasting joy, however, does not exclude us from receiving material blessings. Yet, we cannot forget our spiritual blessings. We have not grown up to the Head in His everlasting joy if we are seeking fulfillment outside of Christ. Material blessings are fleeting and never give the fullness of His everlasting joy. Spiritual blessings are eternal and provide everlasting joy, which sustains us during the most difficult times.

Journal It: Continuing the Growth

Growing up in His everlasting joy does not exclude us from receiving material blessings. However, we cannot forget our spiritual blessings, which are superior to material blessings. Often, when people lose material possessions to natural disasters, they make comments like "We lost everything." But when believers face such disasters, we should know that we haven't lost everything. We still have our spiritual blessings, which include our everlasting joy. How has God's everlasting joy sustained you in times of trouble?

His joy was all that I had.
Without it I would have been
in terrible shape. His joy is what
made me want to continue my journey

Journal It: Continuing the Growth

_____
_____
_____
_____
_____
_____
_____
_____
_____
_____
_____
_____
_____
_____
_____
_____
_____
_____
_____
_____
_____
_____
_____
_____
_____
_____
_____
_____
_____
_____

Week 1 ♦ Day 3

Spiritual Truth:

God's spiritual blessings are countless.

Memory Verse:

"Blessed be the God and Father of our Lord Jesus Christ, who hath blessed us with all spiritual blessings in heavenly places in Christ" (Ephesians 1:3).

Reading Reference:

"Blessed be the God and Father of our Lord Jesus Christ, who hath blessed us with all spiritual blessings in heavenly places in Christ: According as he hath chosen us in him before the foundation of the world, that we should be holy and without blame before him in love: Having predestined us unto the adoption of children by Jesus Christ to himself, according to the good pleasure of his will, to the praise of the glory of his grace, wherein he hath made us accepted in the beloved. In whom we have redemption through his blood, the forgiveness of sins, according to the riches of his grace; Wherein he hath abounded toward us in all wisdom and prudence; Having made known unto us the mystery of his will, according to his good pleasure which he hath purposed in himself: That in the dispensation of the fullness of

Week 1 ◆ Day 3

"times he might gather together in one all things in Christ, both which are in heaven, and which are on earth; even in him: In whom also we have obtained an inheritance, being predestined according to the purpose of him who worketh all things after the counsel of his own will: That we should be to the praise of his glory, who first trusted Christ. In whom ye also trusted, after that ye heard the word of truth, the gospel of your salvation: in whom also after that ye believed, ye were sealed with that holy Spirit of promise, Which is the earnest of our inheritance until the redemption of the purchased possession, unto the praise of his glory "(Ephesians 1:3–14).

How Do We Grow Up in Everlasting Joy? (Part II)

Again, growing up to the Head in His everlasting joy means placing greater value on spiritual blessings than on material blessings. One way of doing this is by counting our blessings.

In Ephesians 1:3–14, Paul gives us the seven keys to everlasting joy. When we recognize the true worth of these spiritual blessings, the result is growing up in God's everlasting joy. These are the kind of blessings that, as the old folks used to say, "I just couldn't keep it to myself." They are the kind you have to tell somebody about.

We think too much about material blessings and don't talk enough about spiritual blessings. There are some spiritual blessings we need to concentrate on and praise God for. In fact, there are seven blessings that are key to growing up in everlasting joy. You will examine these seven spiritual blessings as part of your *Continuing the Growth* study today.

Journal It: Continuing the Growth

Using the *Reading References* Scriptures on pages 10 and 11, describe how each of the following spiritual blessings enhances your everlasting joy.

Being Chosen (v.4)   Adoption (v.5–6)

Redemption (v.7)   Wisdom (v.8)

Knowing (v.9–10)   Inheritance (v.11)

Sealed (v.13–14)

I. My joy is enhanced because I know that God has a plan for me.

II. Being redeemed means that God forgave me and overlooked my shortcomings. Sealed. done deal.
Being adopted means that I was taken in. A man on a path to destruction and now I have guidance into the light.
Wisdom. Know right from wrong.
Inheritance. I have availability to all that the father have

Week 1 ◆ Day 4

Spiritual Truth:

God does bless materially.

Memory Verse:

"Blessed be the God and Father of our Lord Jesus Christ, who hath blessed us with all spiritual blessings in heavenly places in Christ" (Ephesians 1:3).

Reading References:

"And it shall come to pass, if thou shalt hearken diligently unto the voice of the LORD thy God, to observe and to do all his commandments which I command thee this day, that the LORD thy God will set thee on high above all nations of the earth. And all these blessings shall come on thee, and overtake thee, if thou shalt hearken unto the voice of the LORD thy God. Blessed shalt thou be in the city, and blessed shalt thou be in the field. Blessed shall be the fruit of thy body, and the fruit of thy ground, and the fruit of thy cattle, the increase of thy kine, and the flocks of thy sheep. Blessed shall be thy basket and thy store. Blessed shalt thou be when thou comest in, and blessed shalt thou be when thou goest out. And the LORD shall make thee the head, and not the tail; and thou shalt be above only, and thou shalt not be

Week 1 ◆ Day 4

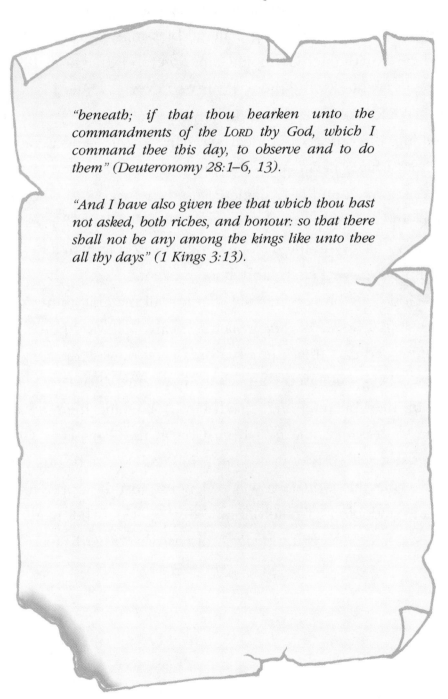

"beneath; if that thou hearken unto the commandments of the LORD thy God, which I command thee this day, to observe and to do them" (Deuteronomy 28:1–6, 13).

"And I have also given thee that which thou hast not asked, both riches, and honour: so that there shall not be any among the kings like unto thee all thy days" (1 Kings 3:13).

God Does Bless Materially

Growing up to the Head in His everlasting joy does not exclude us from receiving material blessings (1 Kings 3:13). When the Summer Olympic Games were in Atlanta in 1996, I really wanted to be there. I pursued every avenue I could, but could not find tickets to any of the games. As I was getting discouraged, a deaf woman, Carol Kent Carson, whom I have never met, sent me four tickets to one of the evening track and field games. I used the tickets to take my son and grandson to the event. It was thrilling for us to observe history in the making. God blessed me with a desire of my heart—tickets to an Olympic event.

God does bless materially, but not all material things are blessings from God. For instance, many believers purchase homes and cars they cannot afford. They praise God for the items they purchased, but when they can't afford to keep them, they become angry with God for taking them away. The truth is that it wasn't from God in the first place. God does not put His people in debt. In fact, He teaches us that if we obey his Word, we will be lenders; just the opposite of being indebted (Deuteronomy 28:1–6, 13). The material blessings of God bring peace, not worry and hardship.

Journal It: Continuing the Growth

As wonderful as material blessings are, if we have grown up in everlasting joy, our desire will be fixed on spiritual blessings. Spiritual blessings are superior to material blessings. James 1:17 reads:

> *Every good gift and every perfect gift is from above, and cometh down from the Father of lights, with whom is no variableness, neither shadow of turning.*

Take an inventory of your material possessions. How can you be certain these things are blessings from God? Are they causing you to be more stressed or more at peace?

Peace

Week 1 ◆ Day 5

Spiritual Truth:

Everlasting joy is not circumstantial.

Memory Verse:

"Blessed be the God and Father of our Lord Jesus Christ, who hath blessed us with all spiritual blessings in heavenly places in Christ" (Ephesians 1:3).

Reading References:

"For which I am an ambassador in bonds: that therein I may speak boldly, as I ought to speak" (Ephesians 6:20).

"Unto the angel of the church of Ephesus write; These things saith he that holdeth the seven stars in his right hand, who walketh in the midst of the seven golden candlesticks; I know thy works, and thy labour, and thy patience, and how thou canst not bear them which are evil: and thou hast tried them which say they are apostles, and are not, and hast found them liars: And hast borne, and hast patience, and for my name's sake hast laboured, and hast not fainted. Nevertheless I have somewhat against thee, because thou hast left thy first love. Remember therefore from whence thou art fallen, and repent, and do the first works; or else I will come unto thee quickly, and will remove thy candlestick out of his place, except thou repent" (Revelation 2:1–5).

The Church at Ephesus

I think it's interesting that a man would write about joy from a jail cell. Paul wrote the letter to the church at Ephesus from a prison cell in Rome (Ephesians 6:20), just as he wrote three other epistles while incarcerated: Philippians, Philemon and Colossians. He didn't write it from a high and lofty place where it's easy to be joyous, but from a jail cell in the city of Ephesus. From a prison cell, he wrote about being one in the body of Christ, then began a praise doxology in which he talks about spiritual blessings in Christ.

Ephesus was a seaport town. Anywhere there's a seaport town, whether it's a big city like Miami, or a little city like Portsmouth, Virginia, such towns carry some baggage with them. Seaport towns don't seek everlasting joy. Theirs is the fleeting pleasure that is rooted in carnality. They are towns of red light districts; towns into which drugs are smuggled.

All kinds of cultic worship took place in the temples at Ephesus, even prostitution in cultic worship. One of the main temples in Ephesus was the Temple of Diana. These saints who once worshipped at the Temple of Diana now went to church at the church of God at Ephesus.

The church at Ephesus had cleaned up most of their immoral acts. There is not a lot written about them engaging in immorality. They had even gotten rid of the false apostles and prophets. They had come out of the world into the fullness of Christ. Yet, there was still a problem in their church:

they had forgotten their first love (Revelations 2:1–5). They had forgotten who first loved them and gave them salvation.

How had they forgotten God? They were praising Him for material blessings more than spiritual blessings, much like our churches today. Many of us are praising God, but when we say, "When the praises go up, the blessings come down," most of us are thinking about a Mercedes in the parking lot, money we have in our pockets, the luxurious house we live in, and the jobs we have—the material blessings that God has bestowed upon us. Growing up in His everlasting joy means thinking more about the spiritual blessings God has given us.

Journal It: Continuing the Growth

In yesterday's journal, you were to list your material possessions. Now that you have determined which of these possessions are gifts from God, how have they caused you to forget about God? Reflecting back on the spiritual blessings from day three, what are some things you can do to make sure your spiritual blessings are honored just as much or even more than your material blessings?

_____

_____

_____

_____

_____

_____

_____

_____

_____

_____

_____

_____

_____

_____

_____

_____

_____

_____

Week 1 ◆ Day 6

Spiritual Truth:

Growing up in everlasting joy is continuous.

Memory Verse:

"These things have I spoken unto you, that my joy might remain in you, and that your joy might be full" (John 15:11).

Reading References:

"And I, if I be lifted up from the earth, will draw all men unto me" (John 12:32).

"That we henceforth be no more children, tossed to and fro, and carried about with every wind of doctrine, by the sleight of men, and cunning craftiness, whereby they lie in wait to deceive; But speaking the truth in love, may grow up into him in all things, which is the head, even Christ: From whom the whole body fitly joined together and compacted by that which every joint supplieth, according to the effectual working in the measure of every part, maketh increase of the body unto the edifying of itself in love" (Ephesians 4:14–16).

29 But they constrained him, saying, Abide with us: for it is toward evening, and the day is far spent. And he went in to tarry with them.

30 And it came to pass, as he sat at meat with them, he took bread, and blessed it, and brake, and gave to them.

31 And their eyes were opened, and they knew him; and he vanished out of their sight.

32 And they said one to another, Did not our heart burn within us, while he talked with us by the way, and while he opened to us the scriptures?

33 And they rose up the same hour, and returned to Jerusalem, and found the eleven gathered together, and them that were with them,

34 Saying, The Lord is risen indeed, and hath appeared to Simon.

35 And they told what things were done in the way, and how he was known of them in breaking of bread.

Acts 1:3-4 (KJV)

3 To whom also he shewed himself alive after his passion by many infallible proofs, being seen of them forty days, and speaking of the things pertaining to the kingdom of God:

4 And, being assembled together with them, commanded them that they should not depart from Jerusalem, but wait for the promise of the Father, which, saith he, ye have heard of me.

God wants everybody to have an Emmaus Road experience

"An Emmaus Road experience is when the Lord draws near an your heart burns."

Problem:

Blinded by doubt, ignorance, and disbelief

Spiritual Truth:

1. They missed the point.

2. The gospel is the light, but the spirit gives sight.

3. God loves us so much that He will draw near us even when we are walking in the wrong direction.

4. God specializes in hope lost and hope found.

5. A changed heart is a flamed head

Sermon

April 3, 2005

Pastor George O. McCalep, Jr.

"Walking in the Wrong Direction After Easter"

Luke 24:13-35 (KJV)

13 And, behold, two of them went that same day to a village called Emmaus, which was from Jerusalem about threescore furlongs.

14 And they talked together of all these things which had happened.

15 And it came to pass, that, while they communed together and reasoned, Jesus himself drew near, and went with them.

16 But their eyes were holden that they should not know him.

17 And he said unto them, What manner of communications are these that ye have one to another, as ye walk, and are sad?

18 And the one of them, whose name was Cleopas, answering said unto him, Art thou only a stranger in Jerusalem, and hast not known the things which are come to pass therein these days?

19 And he said unto them, What things? And they said unto him, Concerning Jesus of Nazareth, which was a prophet mighty in deed and word before God and all the people:

20 And how the chief priests and our rulers delivered him to be condemned to death, and have crucified him.

21 But we trusted that it had been he which should have redeemed Israel: and beside all this, to day is the third day since these things were done.

22 Yea, and certain women also of our company made us astonished, which were early at the sepulchre;

23 And when they found not his body, they came, saying, that they had also seen a vision of angels, which said that he was alive.

24 And certain of them which were with us went to the sepulchre, and found it even so as the women had said: but him they saw not.

25 Then he said unto them, O fools, and slow of heart to believe all that the prophets have spoken:

26 Ought not Christ to have suffered these things, and to enter into his glory?

27 And beginning at Moses and all the prophets, he expounded unto them in all the scriptures the things concerning himself.

28 And they drew nigh unto the village, whither they went: and he made as though he would have gone further.

All Grown Up

How do you know when you are grown up in His everlasting joy? Many believe they have grown up in everlasting joy because they attend Sunday services with a smile, participate in activities, thank the pastor for his sermon or say, "Hi, how are you?" to other believers. But this is far from the truth. Believers who have grown up in His everlasting joy:

- are contagious Christians who witness and are living testimonies. They help produce a full house on Sunday.

- have victory over anger. Anger stifles the Gospel and the Spirit. When people visit a church and find joy instead of anger, they stay and the church grows.

- give God an easy, natural sacrifice of praise. Praise draws others to Christ (John 12:32).

- grow tall in giving and sharing. It is not just the amount of money or time that is given, but the spirit in which it is done. Those who have grown up in everlasting joy view giving and serving as a joyous privilege, not a duty or chore.

- are no longer babes, tossed by every false teaching and deceitful, cunning scheme of men. Instead, they are assured of their oneness with Christ and continue to grow up into Him in all things.

Journal It: Continuing the Growth

Believers who have grown up in everlasting joy fit into the body of Christ according to the effectual working of their part, and increase the body through love (Ephesians 4:14–16). A believer or church that lacks everlasting joy is:

- not excited.
- filled with anger and strife.
- exemplifies little or no praise.
- poor in giving of time, talent, money, love, etc.

Which of these areas is keeping you from experiencing God's everlasting joy? What will you do to change it?

_____

_____

_____

_____

_____

_____

_____

_____

_____

_____

_____

_____

_____

_____

Journal It: Continuing the Growth

_____

_____

_____

_____

_____

_____

_____

_____

_____

_____

_____

_____

_____

_____

_____

_____

_____

_____

_____

_____

_____

_____

_____

_____

_____

_____

_____

_____

_____

_____

Week 1 ◆ Day 7

Spiritual Truth:

Praise is eternal so start practicing now.

Memory Verse:

"These things have I spoken unto you, that my joy might remain in you, and that your joy might be full" (John 15:11).

Reading References:

"And I, if I be lifted up from the earth, will draw all men unto me" (John 12:32).

"That the trial of your faith, being much more precious than of gold that perisheth, though it be tried with fire, might be found unto praise and honour and glory at the appearing of Jesus Christ: Whom having not seen, ye love; in whom, though now ye see him not, yet believing, ye rejoice with joy unspeakable and full of glory: Receiving the end of your faith, even the salvation of your souls" (1 Peter 1:7–9).

The Sacrifice of Praise

Again, believers who have grown up in His everlasting joy give God a sacrifice of praise that is easy and natural at all times. God is worthy and enjoys our praise. Growing up in everlasting joy includes growing up in praise.

Growing up to the Head involves conforming our nature to that of the Head. The apostle Peter explains this growth process in 1 Peter 1:7–9. Part of that process includes being able to see the hand of God at work, even in the most difficult circumstances. Anyone can praise God during good times. We must be conformed to the Head to praise God in the midst of difficulty.

The ability to praise God in all circumstances does not come automatically. When we are unhappy, we tend to not want to praise God. But if we praise Him when times are hard, He will be lifted up. And if He is lifted up, He will also lift us up and draw us, as well as others, closer to Him. According to John 12:32, praise draws others to Christ.

We must stop confusing happiness with joy because when we do, we confuse the temporary with the eternal. The situation that has us unhappy is only temporary, but God's joy is everlasting. We should always praise Him who is eternal.

Praise God for the spiritual blessings we have available to us in Christ. In Christ, we are saved and made righteous. In Christ, we are redeemed and forgiven. In Christ, we have joy and peace that surpasses all understanding. In Christ, we are found faithful and are loved by Him. In Christ, we can raise holy hands that have been in all kinds of places and can now call ourselves saints. Only in Christ have our sins been washed away by the blood of Jesus. Our spiritual blessings are reasons to offer God a sacrifice of praise.

Journal It: Continuing the Growth

At what times of your life have you failed to praise God? Will you fail to praise Him today? Go to church this week with praising God on your mind. Upon your return, reflect on your experience. In what ways was it different than usual?

_____

_____

_____

_____

_____

_____

_____

_____

_____

_____

_____

_____

_____

_____

_____

_____

_____

_____

_____

_____

_____

Reflections

What did God say to you about growing up in His everlasting joy during your study this week?

_____

_____

_____

_____

_____

_____

_____

_____

_____

_____

_____

_____

_____

_____

_____

_____

_____

_____

_____

_____

Reflections

_____

_____

_____

_____

_____

_____

_____

_____

_____

_____

_____

_____

_____

_____

_____

_____

_____

_____

_____

_____

_____

_____

_____

_____

_____

_____

_____

_____

_____

_____

_____

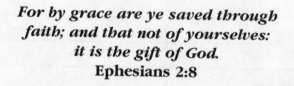

For by grace are ye saved through faith; and that not of yourselves: it is the gift of God.
Ephesians 2:8

And that he might reconcile both unto God in one body by the cross, having slain the enmity thereby.
Ephesians 2:16

Growing Up to the Head in...
Grace and Reconciliation

Acknowledging God

Dear God, I praise You for being a gracious and merciful God. Thank You for the gift of grace. I confess my failure to surrender every area of my life to You. Teach me to surrender everything to You. Help me to grow more in love with You and to always give You all of the glory. I acknowledge you as the reconciler. Thank you for reconciling me to You on Calvary's cross. Lord, tear down all walls that separate me from You. Help me reconcile broken or damaged relationships in my life. Teach me how to remove any walls in my church that may keep someone from knowing Christ. Teach me how to grow up to the Head in Your grace and reconciliation. In Jesus' name. Amen!

Week 2 ◆ Day 1

Spiritual Truth:

God's grace makes you dependent, not independent.

Memory Verse:

"For by grace are ye saved through faith; and that not of yourselves: it is the gift of God" (Ephesians 2:8).

Reading Reference:

"And Jesus called a little child unto him, and set him in the midst of them, And said, Verily I say unto you, Except ye be converted, and become as little children, ye shall not enter into the kingdom of heaven" (Matthew 18:2–3).

What Does It Mean to Grow Up in Grace?

A story has often been told about a father and his five-year-old daughter who went sailing one day. The boat capsized, and the two found themselves stranded in the middle of nowhere. The father decided to attempt to swim back to shore. Before he left his young daughter, he asked her, "Do you remember when Daddy taught you how to float?" She replied, "Yes, Daddy, I remember." Her father instructed her to float there on the water until he returned for her.

The man was found by the Coast Guard. He told them his little girl was still out there. They searched the spot where the boat sunk to no avail. The Coast Guardsmen presumed her to be dead. They tried to console the father. He convinced them to go look for her once more.

This time they found her. Not only was she alive, but she was singing a song! They asked her how she was able to sing although she was stranded. She replied, "My Daddy told me he would come back and get me. My Daddy always keeps his promises."

It takes maturity for a Christian to have as much faith in our Heavenly Father as that five-year-old girl had in her daddy. We have to grow up in grace to have the faith of a child (Matthew 18:2–3).

Grace is God's unmerited favor. It is undeserved goodness that we receive from Him. Growing up in grace means realizing who we are and what we do can never be enough to save us. We are not saved by our deeds. Salvation is a gift from God. It is the opposite of growing up in the world. As we grow up in grace, we become more dependent upon God, not independent. The more we mature as Christians, the greater our dependency upon God should be. Until we become like the little girl in the story, we can never fully experience God's grace.

Journal It: Continuing the Growth

What have you done for God lately? Make a list of the things you have done for God recently. Then, make a list of the things He has done for you. Which list is longer? Do you believe you have earned God's grace based on your list?

_____

_____

_____

_____

_____

_____

_____

_____

_____

_____

_____

_____

_____

_____

_____

_____

_____

_____

_____

_____

Week 2 ◆ Day 2

Spiritual Truth:

God's grace cannot be earned.

Memory Verse:

"For by grace are ye saved through faith; and that not of yourselves: it is the gift of God" (Ephesians 2:8).

Reading Reference:

"Daniel soon proved himself more capable than all the other presidents and governors, for he had great ability, and the king began to think of placing him over the entire empire as his administrative officer. This made the other presidents and governors very jealous, and they began searching for some fault in the way Daniel was handling his affairs so that they could complain to the king about him. But they couldn't find anything to criticize! He was faithful and honest, and made no mistakes" (Daniel 6:3–4 TLB).

Unmerited Favor

In many governmental agencies, people are hired, promoted or paid on what is known as a merit system. That means you earn your way up; either up the chain of command or up the economic ladder. It is a breeding ground for corruption because people earn merits based on conditions other than job performance.

That is probably what would happen if God had a merit system. Can you imagine how corrupt we would try to make it? We would probably go behind one another's backs, trying to kick each other out of favor with God so we could move ourselves in.

When we grow up in His grace, we take comfort in the fact that gaining His favor is not like gaining human favor. That is what happened to Daniel (Daniel 6:3–4). The other high-ranking Babylonian officials were upset because Daniel had favor with King Darius. They thought that by removing Daniel, they would place themselves in a better position to earn favor with the king. Even in that circumstance, because of God's grace, Daniel was spared from the lion's den. God cannot be tricked or fooled. That is why it is best for us to come before Him being straightforward and honest about our shortcomings and inadequacies. We should relax and rejoice over the fact that God loves us so much that He wants to give us the priceless gift of grace. Growing up in grace means that we accept God's gift and leave it alone.

Growing up in His grace begins with realizing how unworthy we are to receive God's grace. As long as we think we have earned some grace, we have some growing up to do. When we try to earn God's favor, we only become frustrated because we are trying to do the impossible. Growing up in grace releases us from trying to earn God's favor.

Journal It: Continuing the Growth

Reflect on what God's grace means to you personally. How is God's grace being exhibited in your life?

_____

_____

_____

_____

_____

_____

_____

_____

_____

_____

_____

_____

_____

_____

_____

_____

_____

_____

_____

_____

_____

_____

Week 2 ◆ Day 3

Spiritual Truth:

Grace and worry are incompatible.

Memory Verse:

"For by grace are ye saved through faith; and that not of yourselves: it is the gift of God" (Ephesians 2:8).

Reading Reference:

"As far as the east is from the west, so far hath he removed our transgressions from us" (Psalm 103:12).

Power of Surrender

There is a story about a little girl who told a priest that she had been speaking to Jesus. The old priest did not believe her, but the child persisted. Finally the priest said, "Okay, the next time you talk to Him, ask Him to tell you what my last sin was." The little girl came back to the priest and said, "I spoke to Jesus and asked Him about your last sin." Curious, the old priest responded, "Really? And what did He tell you?" The child replied, "He said He forgot."

When we surrender to God, all our sins are forgiven and forgotten. God's grace removes our past, present and future sins (Psalm 103:12). It is Satan who tries to imprison us with guilt and shame after Christ has set us free. It is Satan who wants us to think we are not worthy to serve the Lord because of our past. It is also Satan who tries to cripple us with fear about the future. God cannot use us when we are paralyzed with fear.

Grace and worry are incompatible. When worried, fear consumes us and we have **no time** to focus on godly things, **no energy** to devote to the kingdom of God, and **no faith** to see that God has a better plan for our lives. Fear and worry make us think that God is as powerless as we are.

Journal It: Continuing the Growth

In the table below, list those things you worry about in the column labeled "My Worries," and then list your fears in the column labeled "My Fears." Next, bow your head, close your eyes and repeat the following prayer aloud several times: "Lord I give you total control of my life." When you are ready, open your eyes. What did you feel? Hopefully, it was the feeling of complete surrender to God. What went through your mind? Why?

My Worries	My Fears

Week 2 ◆ Day 4

Spiritual Truth:

Jesus Christ tore down every wall that separated you from His love.

Memory Verse:

"And that he might reconcile both unto God in one body by the cross, having slain the enmity thereby" (Ephesians 2:16).

Reading References:

"And, behold, the veil of the temple was rent in twain from the top to the bottom; and the earth did quake, and the rocks rent" (Matthew 27:51).

"And after the second veil, the tabernacle which is called the Holiest of all" (Hebrews 9:3).

"Having therefore, brethren, boldness to enter into the holiest by the blood of Jesus, By a new and living way, which he hath consecrated for us, through the veil, that is to say, his flesh" (Hebrews 10:19–20).

What is Reconciliation?

King Solomon built a temple for God to dwell in. The temple contained the court of the Israelites where the Israelite men offered sacrifices to God. There was also an inner court called the Holy of Holies. No one dared go into that court but the high priest, and even he could only go in during certain times of the year. Before he could enter, he had to undergo a cleansing ritual. The Holy of Holies was separated from the rest of the temple by a curtain (Hebrews 9:3) because it was the place where God dwelled.

The Gospels tell us that when Jesus was crucified, the curtain was torn (Matthew 27:51). It is interesting to note the things Christians pay attention to related to Jesus' crucifixion, including how Mount Sinai reacted, the splitting of the rock, and the sun darkening. Somehow we overlook the fact that when Jesus was crucified, the curtain was torn and reconciliation began (Hebrews 10:19–20). The torn curtain symbolized free access to the Father for all people through Jesus Christ.

Reconciliation re-joins that which was separated. The *American Heritage Dictionary*[2] defines *reconcile* as "to re-establish friendship between; to settle or resolve, as a dispute; to bring (oneself) to accept; to make compatible or consistent." Growing up in reconciliation means to tear down every wall or partition that separates us from being fully reconciled to Jesus Christ.

---

2. *The American Heritage Dictionary, S*eond College Edition, s.v. "Reconcile."

Journal It: Continuing the Growth

Who were you before being reconciled to God? How has being reconciled with God changed your life?

_____

_____

_____

_____

_____

_____

_____

_____

_____

_____

_____

_____

_____

_____

_____

_____

_____

_____

_____

_____

_____

_____

Week 2 ◆ Day 5

Spiritual Truth:

You cannot hate others and have a right relationship with God.

Memory Verse:

"And that he might reconcile both unto God in one body by the cross, having slain the enmity thereby" (Ephesians 2:16).

Reading References:

"Therefore if thou bring thy gift to the altar, and there rememberest that thy brother hath ought against thee; Leave there thy gift before the altar, and go thy way; first be reconciled to thy brother, and then come and offer thy gift" (Matthew 5:23–24).

"Moreover if thy brother shall trespass against thee, go and tell him his fault between thee and him alone: if he shall hear thee, thou hast gained thy brother. But if he will not hear thee, then take with thee one or two more, that in the mouth of two or three witnesses every word may be established" (Matthew 18:15–16).

Week 2 ◆ Day 5

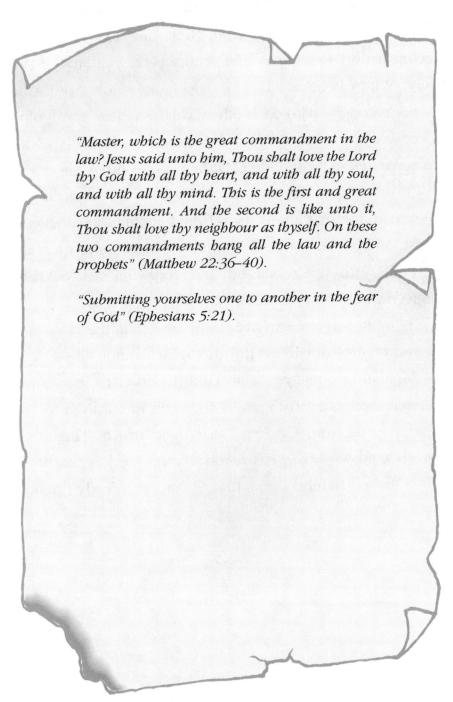

"Master, which is the great commandment in the law? Jesus said unto him, Thou shalt love the Lord thy God with all thy heart, and with all thy soul, and with all thy mind. This is the first and great commandment. And the second is like unto it, Thou shalt love thy neighbour as thyself. On these two commandments hang all the law and the prophets" (Matthew 22:36–40).

"Submitting yourselves one to another in the fear of God" (Ephesians 5:21).

How Do We Grow Up in Reconciliation?

Jesus Christ opened the door to salvation. Salvation automatically reconciles us to God, but not to each other. Reconciliation with each other occurs as we yield to the Holy Spirit. When believers fail to yield to the Holy Spirit, they cannot reconcile with each other. This recreates a wall of sin because when we are separated from each other, it is sin and sin separates us from God (Matthew 22:36–40).

Christians should seek to remove every obstacle and every partition that keeps them from becoming reconciled to Christ. All believers should submit to each other as unto God and be kind, tenderhearted and forgiving, as God has forgiven us (Ephesians 5:21).

The only way we can live this is by letting the Holy Spirit fill and control our lives. But the Spirit cannot fill us, if we are separating ourselves from God. In order to grow up in reconciliation, we must identify the walls in our lives that are separating us from God and tear them down. Those who have not grown up in His reconciliation are keeping themselves locked behind doors that Christ has already opened.

Journal It: Continuing the Growth

What broken or damaged relationships are in your life? If you are not sure, ask the Holy Spirit to reveal those relationships to you and to guide you in reconciling them. Matthew 5:23–24 instructs us to agree with those we are in conflict with quickly. Matthew 18:15–16 instructs us to seek reconciliation again and again, if our first attempt is not successful.

_____

_____

_____

_____

_____

_____

_____

_____

_____

_____

_____

_____

_____

_____

_____

_____

_____

Week 2 ◆ Day 6

Spiritual Truth:

God sees your invisible walls.

Memory Verse:

"And that he might reconcile both unto God in one body by the cross, having slain the enmity thereby" (Ephesians 2:16).

Reading References:

"And, behold, the veil of the temple was rent in twain from the top to the bottom; and the earth did quake, and the rocks rent" (Matthew 27:51).

"And the sun was darkened, and the veil of the temple was rent in the midst" (Luke 23:45).

Tearing Down Invisible Walls

The curtain that was torn down at Jesus' death was a real curtain (Matthew 27:51, Luke 23:45). There were real walls in the temple which designated various divisions. But real walls are not the only types of barriers.

Invisible walls are more damaging than physical walls. A person can devise a way to get around or through a physical wall. However, we cannot do that with invisible walls. Invisible walls are dangerous because we may not know they are there, nor do we know how high, wide or thick the wall is. If we can't see the walls, we do not know what we are up against. We can't see them, but God can.

Sometimes we create invisible walls. We may even build walls to keep others out, not realizing that we are forcing ourselves to stay in. Growing up in reconciliation means picking up a sledge hammer and breaking down all walls that separate us from God, including personal walls. Some of us are afraid to take the sledge hammer to our own walls.

Jesus has given us a finished and complete plan of reconciliation, but we continue to build walls that separate men from God, women from God, women from women, men from men, and men and women from each other. Some of the greatest battles in the church are due to issues of gender.

There are social or class walls that separate us: the haves from the have-nots; the upper class from the middle class; and the middle class from the lower class. Others may not see our invisible walls, but God always sees everything.

Journal It: Continuing the Growth

Ask the Holy Spirit to reveal invisible walls in your life. Do any of the walls mentioned previously apply to your life situation? If so, surrender them to God today and be reconciled. If not, praise God for freedom from invisible walls.

_____

_____

_____

_____

_____

_____

_____

_____

_____

_____

_____

_____

_____

_____

_____

_____

_____

_____

_____

Week 2 ◆ Day 7

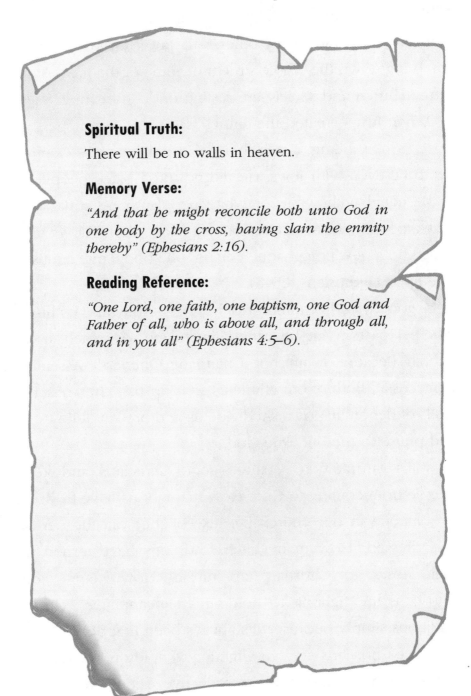

Spiritual Truth:

There will be no walls in heaven.

Memory Verse:

"And that he might reconcile both unto God in one body by the cross, having slain the enmity thereby" (Ephesians 2:16).

Reading Reference:

"One Lord, one faith, one baptism, one God and Father of all, who is above all, and through all, and in you all" (Ephesians 4:5–6).

Tearing Down Load-Bearing Walls

In the construction industry, there are "load-bearing" walls that look the same as any other wall, but if torn down, they can bring down the whole structure. Some of the greatest ills in the church and society are resting on load-bearing walls.

When Jesus created the church, He made a new person-hood, a new being, a new body. He did not raise Gentiles up to be even with Jews. He did not raise black people up to be equal with white or white people to be equal with black people. Instead, He melted all of them down and raised up a new being—one person, one body, one baptism, one Spirit (Ephesians 4:5–6).

A good friend of mine preaches beautifully at the church where I pastor, but he cannot invite me to preach at his church because I am not Unitarian (Oneness) Assembly Pentecostal. Both of our churches are Christian churches, but walls of denominationalism divide us and prevent fellowship and praise to the one true God.

Walls of tradition separate good Christians and keep people from coming to God. How many of us have frowned at someone in our church because of the way the person was dressed? How many older Christians have turned up their noses to Christian rap music? How many older Christians are fighting to hold on to meaningless, church traditions simply because "It's always been that way"?

Some Christians are even fighting to hold on to traditions that are oppressive or counterproductive. Yet, we hold on to those traditions. We fight for them. We are even willing to leave a church for them! How many of us would fight so strongly to hold on so dearly to Christ?

God is calling today's church to break down the walls of racism, tradition, denominationalism and any other obstacle that prevents a person from coming to God. Christ tore down every wall that separates us from Him, and when He returns and takes us home, none of the walls we have created between each other will exist in our heavenly home.

Journal It: Continuing the Growth

Have you allowed load-bearing walls to surround you? If so, what are they? Racism? Denominationalism? Traditions? What is the first step you need to take to demolish these walls?

_____

_____

_____

_____

_____

_____

_____

_____

_____

_____

_____

_____

_____

_____

_____

_____

_____

_____

_____

_____

_____

Reflections

Reflect on your time with God this week. What did God say to you about growing up in His grace and reconciliation?

_____

_____

_____

_____

_____

_____

_____

_____

_____

_____

_____

_____

_____

_____

_____

_____

_____

_____

_____

_____

_____

_____

_____

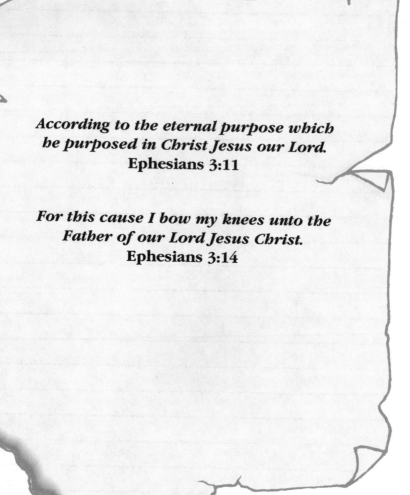

According to the eternal purpose which he purposed in Christ Jesus our Lord.
Ephesians 3:11

For this cause I bow my knees unto the Father of our Lord Jesus Christ.
Ephesians 3:14

Growing Up to the Head in...
Purpose & Prayer

Acknowledging God

Dear God, I acknowledge You as the God of purpose and prayer. I praise You for being the divine Architect of my life. Thank You for giving me victory over all things that separate me from You. Thank You for Your divine plan. I ask that the Holy Spirit reveal Your divine purpose for my life. Help me to put aside my agenda and join You in Yours. Father, I also ask that You teach me how to pray so that my life will be a life of prayer. I thank You for Your Spirit who intercedes for me when I do not know what to pray. Now, unto You, my Lord, who is able to do exceeding abundantly beyond all that I can ask or think, may Your power work in me. Teach me how to grow up to the Head in Your purpose and prayer. In Your name, Lord Jesus, I give You thanks. Amen!

Week 3 ◆ Day 1

Spiritual Truth:

Your life has purpose.

Memory Verse:

"According to the eternal purpose which he purposed in Christ Jesus our Lord" (Ephesians 3:11).

Reading Reference:

"Whereof I was made a minister, according to the gift of the grace of God given unto me by the effectual working of his power. Unto me, who am less than the least of all saints, is this grace given, that I should preach among the Gentiles the unsearchable riches of Christ; And to make all men see what is the fellowship of the mystery, which from the beginning of the world hath been hid in God, who created all things by Jesus Christ: To the intent that now unto the principalities and powers in heavenly places might be known by the church the manifold wisdom of God. According to the eternal purpose which he purposed in Christ Jesus our Lord" (Ephesians 3:7–11).

God's Purpose for the Church

God has gifted His Church for His purpose. Yet, many local churches may not be operating in accordance with that purpose. In fact, they may not have a biblical clue as to what they are supposed to be doing.

A survey was done to determine the number of Christians who knew the biblical purpose of the church. The sad commentary was that only three out of ten pastors of mainline churches today knew the biblical purpose of the church. If the number of clergy was that low, imagine where the laypersons fell in the survey. Actually, they were not that far behind. Only one out of ten church members knew the purpose of the church as God has given it in the Bible.

God has charged the church with a five-fold purpose: worship, fellowship, discipleship, evangelism and ministry/ service. Each of us is an important part of His plan. We belong to God. He saved us for a reason.

The reason many Christians, individually and collectively, have no joy and no peace is because they have no purpose. When unfulfilled people come together, they form unfulfilled groups. A church that is filled with discontented people will be a discontented church.

Ephesians 3:7–11, explains that God had a plan and purpose all along, although He did not reveal it for thousands of years. His perfect plan was not revealed until the proper time. Each of us is an important part of God's plan. We are saved for a reason.

Journal It: Continuing the Growth

What purpose has God revealed for your life? How did God reveal His purpose to you? Has your understanding of His purpose for you evolved over time, or did you understand it right away?

_____

_____

_____

_____

_____

_____

_____

_____

_____

_____

_____

_____

_____

_____

_____

_____

_____

_____

_____

_____

Week 3 ◆ Day 2

Spiritual Truth:

The Holy Spirit has given you at least one spiritual gift.

Memory Verse:

"According to the eternal purpose which he purposed in Christ Jesus our Lord" (Ephesians 3:11).

Reading References:

"But the fruit of the Spirit is love, joy, peace, longsuffering, gentleness, goodness, faith, meekness, temperance: against such there is no law" (Galatians 5:22–23).

"Wherefore he saith, when he ascended up on high, he led captivity captive, and gave gifts unto men. (Now that he ascended, what is it but that he also descended first into the lower parts of the earth? He that descended is the same also that ascended up far above all heavens, that he might fill all things.) And he gave some, apostles; and some, prophets; and some, evangelists; and some, pastors and teachers; for the perfecting of the saints, for the work of the ministry, for the edifying of the body of Christ" (Ephesians 4:8–12).

Additional Reading Reference:

1 Corinthians 12–14

Gifted for the Task

Growing up in His purpose means growing up in His spiritual gifts. Not only does God save us from something, He also saves us for something. The Holy Spirit gives each believer at least one spiritual gift when he/she is saved. Ephesians 4:8–12 proclaims that in every believer's gift there is a three-fold purpose: perfecting the saints, work of ministry and edifying the body of Christ. One of the problems in identifying our spiritual gifts is that many believers tend to confuse spiritual gifts with things they are not. Do NOT confuse spiritual gifts with:

- **Talents:** Talents may indicate our spiritual gifts, but they are not necessarily the same as our spiritual gifts. We are born with natural talents. The Holy Spirit gives us spiritual gifts when we are re-born.

- **Fruit of the Spirit:** The fruit of the Spirit is love, joy, peace, patience, kindness, goodness, faithfulness, gentleness and self-control (Galatians 5:22–23). These qualities mark the presence and maturity of the Holy Spirit within a believer. Fruit has to do with our character, "who we are." Spiritual gifts are related to "what we do with who we are."

- **Spiritual Disciplines:** Bible study, prayer, fasting, tithing and other practices are disciplines that help us grow in our relationship with God. They grow our faith, self-control and character.

- **Ministry Positions:** A title such as pastor, teacher or leader may or may not match your spiritual gift. For example, some small group leaders may have the gift of shepherding or encouraging. Titles communicate the functions people fulfill. Their spiritual gifts are seen in what they do as they perform the function.

Journal It: Continuing the Growth

All Christians are spiritually gifted. Every believer has been given a spiritual gift. Every believer is called to a ministry task. Find your spiritual gift, and you will find your ministry. To learn more about spiritual gifts, read 1 Corinthians 12–14. What is your spiritual gift? Are you using it? If not, why not?

_____

_____

_____

_____

_____

_____

_____

_____

_____

_____

_____

_____

_____

_____

_____

_____

_____

_____

Week 3 ◆ Day 3

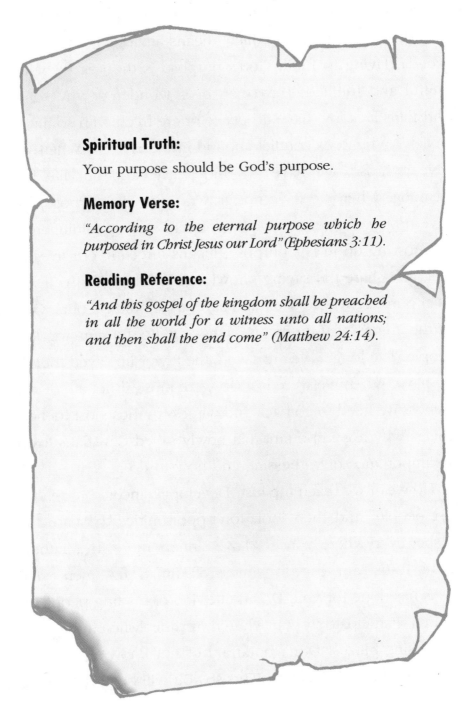

Spiritual Truth:

Your purpose should be God's purpose.

Memory Verse:

"According to the eternal purpose which he purposed in Christ Jesus our Lord" (Ephesians 3:11).

Reading Reference:

"And this gospel of the kingdom shall be preached in all the world for a witness unto all nations; and then shall the end come" (Matthew 24:14).

How Do We Grow Up in His Purpose?

To find our purpose, we have to find out what Jesus' agenda is and join Him in it, which means giving up our own agenda. Living to fulfill God's purpose is the key to being fruitful and fulfilled. Have you ever wondered why some Christians lack joy, have no peace or are filled with so much anxiety? Why does conflict abound in the church? When we have purpose, we have joy and peace, and our life has meaning. When we have not grown up in His purpose, we have no joy, no peace, no contentment and no fulfillment.

Growing up in His purpose, means directing our lives to seek and share the saving knowledge of Jesus Christ. Jesus' focal purpose was to seek and save, as should be ours. One of the things that hurts us is having no burden for lost people. The longer we are saved, the fewer un-saved friends we have. When we were lost, so were most, if not all, of our friends. We need to go back and witness to those lost friends. This is why it is important that newly saved Christians learn the importance of witnessing and how to do it.

How can we reach the lost? Develop a sincere burden for lost people, and then look for opportunities to share the gospel everywhere you go. Love sinners more. In Matthew 24:14, Jesus said to be a witness of Him. Tell sinners what Jesus has done for you. Do a better job of inviting people to church. Participate in your church's evangelistic efforts, e.g., witnessing blitzes. Don't be afraid of not knowing answers to all questions, but get answers so you will be prepared the next time.

Growing up to His purpose means accepting that God chose us according to His divine knowledge—knowledge to which we are not privy. As we think of Moses, we think of what he became, not how he began. We forget that Moses had to go to Pharoah twelve times before the Israelites were freed from bondage. It is important to remember that just because we have to keep trying does not mean that God is not with us. Equally important to remember is that God's purpose will ultimately be fulfilled, no matter who tries to get in the way. Growing up in His purpose means to "keep on keeping on" in spite of obstacles.

God is our divine Architect. He has a perfect plan for each of us. We may fear that yielding to His purpose is dangerous because we don't know where we might end up, but growing up in His purpose is only dangerous if we do not trust Him. If we lose ourselves to Him and His purpose, we gain eternal life and we grow up in Him.

Journal It: Continuing the Growth

How are you fulfilling your God-given purpose? Does your purpose align with God's five-fold purpose for the church?

_____

_____

_____

_____

_____

_____

_____

_____

_____

_____

_____

_____

_____

_____

_____

_____

_____

_____

_____

_____

_____

Week 3 ◆ Day 4

Spiritual Truth:

You must be rooted and grounded in prayer.

Memory Verse:

"For this cause I bow my knees unto the Father of our Lord Jesus Christ" (Ephesians 3:14).

Reading References:

"That Christ may dwell in your hearts by faith; that ye, being rooted and grounded in love" (Ephesians 3:17).

"Now unto him that is able to do exceeding abundantly above all that we ask or think, according to the power that worketh in us" (Ephesians 3:20).

Growing Up in Prayer: Having Deep Roots

Pine trees, although tall and beautiful, do not have a good root system. They can be blown over as soon as a strong wind comes along, unlike the sequoia trees of Northern California. Sequoias have a great root system, which make them big and let them live a long time. Their roots spread and tie in with other sequoia trees so when the wind blows and storms come, they are anchored by their roots.

Christians could learn a great deal from the sequoia trees. When strong winds of tribulation try to knock us down, we should draw upon the strength of each other. We should be anchored in our roots and stick together like the sequoias.

Growing up in prayer means developing deep roots. In Ephesians 3:17, Paul prays for us to be "rooted and grounded" in love. If a church and her membership are rooted and grounded in love and prayer, an occasional wrong decision will not leave the body devastated. The church will survive because the members hold onto and strengthen each other in love.

Growing up in prayer means developing deep roots so that when trouble comes, we are anchored and not blown away. Growing up in prayer means knowing that God is able to do exceeding abundantly beyond all that we ask, think or imagine (Ephesians 3:20). Growing up in prayer also means knowing the purpose of answered prayer is to glorify God through Jesus Christ. Lastly, growing up in prayer means the more we pray, the more we learn about how to pray.

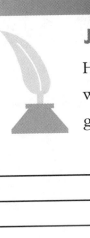

Journal It: Continuing the Growth

How can growing up in prayer help you weather the strong winds of tribulation? How can growing up in prayer help your church?

_____

_____

_____

_____

_____

_____

_____

_____

_____

_____

_____

_____

_____

_____

_____

_____

_____

_____

_____

_____

_____

_____

Week 3 ◆ Day 5

Spiritual Truth:

You should always pray with the right motive.

Memory Verse:

"For this cause I bow my knees unto the Father of our Lord Jesus Christ" (Ephesians 3:14).

Reading References:

"And when thou prayest, thou shalt not be as the hypocrites are: for they love to pray standing in the synagogues and in the corners of the streets, that they may be seen of men. Verily I say unto you, They have their reward. But thou, when thou prayest, enter into thy closet, and when thou hast shut thy door, pray to thy Father which is in secret; and thy Father which seeth in secret shall reward thee openly. But when ye pray, use not vain repetitions, as the heathen do: for they think that they shall be heard for their much speaking. Be not ye therefore like unto them: for your Father knoweth what things ye have need of, before ye ask him" (Matthew 6:5–8.).

Week 3 ◆ Day 5

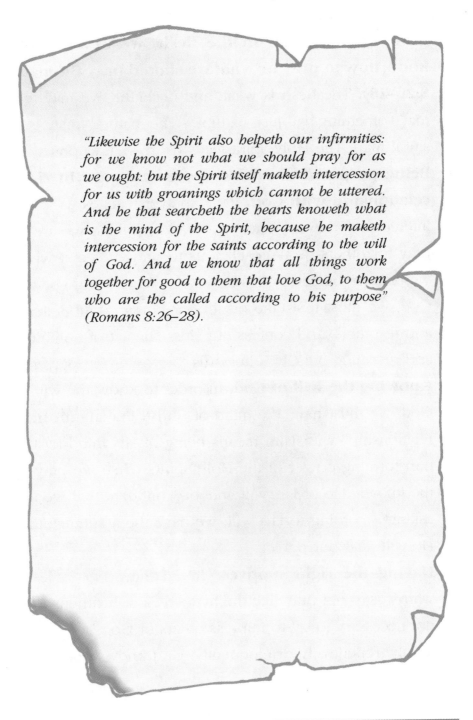

"Likewise the Spirit also helpeth our infirmities: for we know not what we should pray for as we ought: but the Spirit itself maketh intercession for us with groanings which cannot be uttered. And he that searcheth the hearts knoweth what is the mind of the Spirit, because he maketh intercession for the saints according to the will of God. And we know that all things work together for good to them that love God, to them who are the called according to his purpose" (Romans 8:26–28).

Knowing How to Pray

Knowing how to pray means:

- **Understanding that in the flesh, we never really know how to pray or what we should pray (Romans 8:26–28).** The flesh is weak and deceitful. We may feel that something is "just natural." The natural man is a sinful man. The Holy Spirit leads us in what to pray.

- **Being prepared, available vessels that are in right relationship with God.** Paul's prayer teaches us about intercessory prayer. When we pray in public, we are to pray for others. Jesus teaches us to pray in secret when we pray for ourselves (Matthew 6:6). When we go before God, we must first take off all our human doubts, fears and restraints, and confess our sins. The act of humbling and revealing ourselves helps us to grow up in prayer.

- **Knowing the will of God.** In order to know the will of God, we must have the mind of Christ. Praying in "right relationship" with Him means being of His mind by the transforming power of the Holy Spirit. When we pray in the knowledge of His will and are confident that we are asking according to His will, we have the assurance that He will hear our prayer.

- **Having the right motives.** In Matthew 6:5–8, Jesus warns us to not pray like the hypocrites or heathens. It is not necessary to try to impress others or God by praying loudly, repetitively or eloquently. God knows our hearts and our needs.

Journal It: Continuing the Growth

God wants us to know how to pray. He teaches us how to pray in His Word. Growing up in prayer is praying with authority and power. It is praying the way God teaches us, in accordance to His Word and based on His promises. There is no other way.

List everything and everyone you are feeling led to pray for. Then, think about what you just read as a guide for your prayer. Lastly, write out your prayer, and then pray it. The more you pray, the more you learn how to pray.

_____
_____
_____
_____
_____
_____
_____
_____
_____
_____
_____
_____
_____
_____
_____

Journal It: Continuing the Growth

Week 3 ◆ Day 6

Spiritual Truth:

Praying for the internal will help your external to line up with God's plan for your life.

Memory Verse:

"For this cause I bow my knees unto the Father of our Lord Jesus Christ" (Ephesians 3:14).

Reading Reference:

"That he would grant you, according to the riches of his glory, to be strengthened with might by his Spirit in the inner man; that Christ may dwell in your hearts by faith; that ye, being rooted and grounded in love, may be able to comprehend with all saints what is the breadth, and length, and depth, and height; and to know the love of Christ, which passeth knowledge, that ye might be filled with all the fulness of God" (Ephesians 3:16–19).

Knowing What to Pray For

In Ephesians 3:16–19, Paul makes six petitions that we should use as a model in our prayers:

- Strength and power for the inner being (v.16)
- Christ to rule and reign within our hearts (v.17)
- Being rooted and grounded in love (v.17)
- Knowing the love of God (v.18–19)
- Understanding of spiritual truths (v.19)
- The fullness of God (v.19)

Notice, every petition is for something within, something for the inner being. Paul's prayer is for every believer to have an indwelling of God. Nowhere in his prayer does Paul pray for material things. He doesn't pray for cars, homes, job, etc. Those are acceptable prayer requests, but they are not found in this prayer. Paul's prayer is for the inner being to be strengthened, to have an understanding of spiritual things, and to experience the fullness of God.

We need to have Christ's mind, heart and nature. While God lives in all saints, He is not at home in all saints. Our challenge is to make our hearts His home. Many of us never pray for our inner being because our external needs consume us. Growing up to the Head in prayer means giving more attention to your inner self. Growing up in prayer means praying for change within. After all, that is where change occurs.

Journal It: Continuing the Growth

Are the things you normally pray for internal or external? Are these things in line with God's plan for your life? Write a prayer for the inner being of other believers and yourself, and then pray it.

_____

_____

_____

_____

_____

_____

_____

_____

_____

_____

_____

_____

_____

_____

_____

_____

_____

_____

_____

_____

_____

_____

Week 3 ◆ Day 7

Spiritual Truth:

You should pray about everything.

Memory Verse:

"For this cause I bow my knees unto the Father of our Lord Jesus Christ" (Ephesians 3:14).

Reading References:

"I have set watchmen upon thy walls, O Jerusalem, which shall never hold their peace day nor night: ye that make mention of the LORD, keep not silence, And give him no rest, till he establish, and till he make Jerusalem a praise in the earth. The LORD hath sworn by his right hand, and by the arm of his strength, Surely I will no more give thy corn to be meat for thine enemies; and the sons of the stranger shall not drink thy wine, for the which thou hast laboured" (Isaiah 62:6–8).

"Moreover when ye fast, be not, as the hypocrites, of a sad countenance: for they disfigure their faces, that they may appear unto men to fast. Verily I say unto you, They have their reward" (Matthew 6:16).

An Old Testament Intercessory Model

In Isaiah 62:6–8, God appoints one hundred sixty-seven watchmen on the walls of Zion to make intercessory prayer for the establishment of God's kingdom on earth and for the glory of Jerusalem. They are watching, praying, fasting and working. He tells them to take no rest, to pray constantly and give Him no rest until He fulfills His promises.

What do we learn from this model? Those who watched and prayed put arms and legs on their prayers. We pray for God to visit the hospitals, homeless shelters and prisons, but we are the arms and legs He has sent to go. They watched, fasted and prayed. Believers should always be alert, but not worried. Believers should also fast and pray when led by the Holy Spirit to do so.

In Matthew 6:16, Jesus said to the disciples, *"When you pray..."* not *"If you pray."* They prayed without ceasing, and they prayed according to God's promises. Their constant prayers reminded God and the people of God's promises. It is not that God needs reminding. God knows what He promised. However, He enjoys our relationship with Him. He wants us to know His promises.

The Israelites praised God in their prayers. We grieve God with our "gimme" prayers. We need to praise God in our prayers for who He is and what He has done for us. Believers who have grown up to the Head in prayer know that we must praise God when we pray.

Finally, the Israelites prayed for provision so they would be able to do. If there is anything that the devil does not want us to know, it is the able-ness of God. God has already given us the power to do whatever because He is able to do whatever. A mature believer knows that it is not the outer condition, but the inner being that is most important.

Journal It: Continuing the Growth

Is your prayer life consistent? Do you pray about every aspect of your life? Like the one hundred sixty-seven watchmen, are there usually benefactors of your prayers besides you, your family and friends?

_____

_____

_____

_____

_____

_____

_____

_____

_____

_____

_____

_____

_____

_____

_____

_____

_____

_____

_____

_____

_____

Reflections

What did God say to you this week about growing up in His purpose? What did He say to you about growing up in prayer?

_____
_____
_____
_____
_____
_____
_____
_____
_____
_____
_____
_____
_____
_____
_____
_____
_____
_____
_____
_____
_____
_____

Reflections

_____

_____

_____

_____

_____

_____

_____

_____

_____

_____

_____

_____

_____

_____

_____

_____

_____

_____

_____

_____

_____

_____

_____

_____

_____

_____

_____

_____

_____

_____

_____

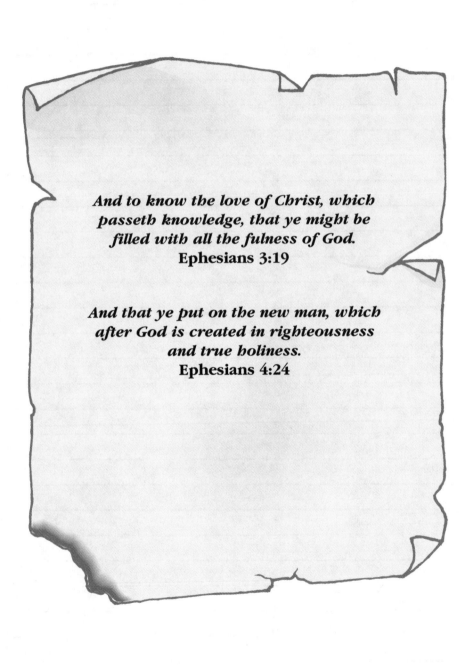

And to know the love of Christ, which passeth knowledge, that ye might be filled with all the fulness of God.
Ephesians 3:19

And that ye put on the new man, which after God is created in righteousness and true holiness.
Ephesians 4:24

Growing Up to the Head in...
His Love & Likeness

Acknowledging God

Dear God, today I acknowledge You as the God of love and the God I want to be like. I pray today that You grow me up in Your love and likeness. It is my desire to put on the new man that is within me, and to shed the old man within me daily. As You loved the world, teach me to love others. Teach me to grow in Your love and Your likeness—righteous and holy. I know that I cannot be You, but it is my desire to be a great imitator of You: to serve, give and love just like You. Teach me how to grow up to the Head in Your love and likeness. In Your name, Lord Jesus, I give You thanks. Amen!

Week 4 ◆ Day 1

Spiritual Truth:

Love is what you do.

Memory Verse:

"And to know the love of Christ, which passeth knowledge, that ye might be filled with all the fulness of God" (Ephesians 3:19).

Reading References:

"For God so loved the world, that he gave his only begotten son, that whosoever believeth in him should not perish, but have everlasting life" (John 3:16).

"If ye love me, keep my commandments" (John 14:15).

Love in Action

Is the love of Christ in your "heart" or in your "head"? Most know who God is because we read the Bible. God loves us, and we are to love Him. We know how He gave His only begotten Son for us. John 3:16 describes Jesus' love in action for us. But do we truly love God with our hearts or just with our head knowledge? If we really love Him, we will have a monogamous relationship with Him because pleasing Him will be more important to us than pleasing others.

Growing up in God's love means experiencing and sharing His love. Everything we do as disciples should hinge on God's love. Every relationship we have should hinge on His love. Growing up in God's love means knowing that God wants us to love Him not just with our heads and lip service, but also with our hearts and actions (John 14:15).

In Ephesians 3:19, Paul talks about the love of Christ. In the Greek language, there are three types of love: eros, philos and agape. *Eros* love is physical, sexual or romantic love. The joy of eros love, even in the best of marriages, is short-lived. Human beings are not sustained on a love that simply, "turns me on." *Philos* love is mutual love. Philos love says, "I love you as long as you love me." It is conditional. *Agape* love is unconditional love. Agape love says, "I love you no matter what." Agape love only comes from God. Human beings who are controlled by the flesh cannot give agape love. Agape love is the love that Paul prayed for us to know in Ephesians 3:19.

Journal It: Continuing the Growth

Which type of love do you desire to experience throughout your life? Which type of love do you usually show to others? How does growing up to the Head in His love affect your relationships with family, co-workers, friends, church members and strangers? What adjustments do you need to make?

_____

_____

_____

_____

_____

_____

_____

_____

_____

_____

_____

_____

_____

_____

_____

_____

_____

_____

_____

_____

_____

_____

Week 4 ◆ Day 2

Spiritual Truth:

God is love.

Memory Verse:

"And to know the love of Christ, which passeth knowledge, that ye might be filled with all the fulness of God" (Ephesians 3:19).

Reading References:

"Then one of them, which was a lawyer, asked him a question, tempting him, and saying, Master, which is the great commandment in the law? Jesus said unto him, Thou shalt love the Lord thy God with all thy heart, and with all thy soul, and with all thy mind. This is the first and great commandment. And the second is like unto it, Thou shalt love thy neighbour as thyself. On these two commandments hang all the law and the prophets" (Matthew 22:35–40).

Week 4 ◆ Day 2

Reading References:

"Though I speak with the tongues of men and of angels, and have not charity, I am become as sounding brass, or a tinkling cymbal. And though I have the gift of prophecy, and understand all mysteries, and all knowledge; and though I have all faith, so that I could remove mountains, and have not charity, I am nothing. And though I bestow all my goods to feed the poor; and though I give my body to be burned, and have not charity, it profiteth me nothing" *(1 Corinthians 13:1–3).*

The Greatest Gift

Growing up in His love means growing up in God because God is love. Love is the greatest gift God has given us. According to Matthew 22:35–40, Jesus told a lawyer that the greatest commandment is to love God, and the second greatest is to love our neighbor as we love ourselves. Love is who saved us. Love is whom we must commune with and grow up to daily.

Many people read 1 Corinthians 13 as part of their marriage vows, but the context of the chapter really deals with spiritual gifts. Paul is saying that it doesn't matter what gifts we have been given, if love does not motivate us to use those gifts, they are worth nothing. A woman may have the voice of a songbird, yet if she does not love, her gift is worthless. A man may have the gift of serving others, but if he does not love, his gift is worthless. Love is who should be operating in us when we use our spiritual gifts. Love should decide when we use our spiritual gifts, not us.

In Paul's discourse on love (1 Corinthians 13), a lot of the gifts started out together, but love ended up being the champion. In the first round, speaking in tongues was eliminated. In another round, the gift of prophecy was eliminated. There are many gifts, but the final three—faith, hope and love—are lasting gifts. And of these, the greatest is love.

Journal It: Continuing the Growth

Growing up to the Head in love is a continual process. Knowing how God exhibited His love for you, how are you sharing that love with others?

_____

_____

_____

_____

_____

_____

_____

_____

_____

_____

_____

_____

_____

_____

_____

_____

_____

_____

_____

_____

_____

_____

_____

Week 4 ◆ Day 3

Spiritual Truth:

Gifts should be shared lovingly.

Memory Verse:

"And to know the love of Christ, which passeth knowledge, that ye might be filled with all the fulness of God" (Ephesians 3:19).

Reading References:

"Though I speak with the tongues of men and of angels, and have not charity, I am become as sounding brass, or a tinkling cymbal. And though I have the gift of prophecy, and understand all mysteries, and all knowledge; and though I have all faith, so that I could remove mountains, and have not charity, I am nothing. And though I bestow all my goods to feed the poor, and though I give my body to be burned, and have not charity, it profiteth me nothing" (1 Corinthians 13:1–3).

"He saith unto him the third time, Simon, son of Jonas, lovest thou me? Peter was grieved because he said unto him the third time, Lovest thou me? And he said unto him, Lord, thou knowest all things; thou knowest that I love thee. Jesus saith unto him, Feed my sheep" (John 21:17).

Sharing Our Gifts

We (the church) are not using all that God has given us. We hoard our gifts and do not share them in love (1 Corinthians 13:1–3). God loved the world so much that He gave His only Son. He loves us enough to give us spiritual gifts and talents. Surely, we can love Him enough to give those gifts and talents in His service.

The problem is that we want to use our spiritual gifts as we want, not as He wants. God does not permit discrimination. He does not allow us to pick and choose when we share our gifts or with whom. Growing up to the Head in His love means not using God's gifts in a discriminatory manner.

Too many church members have gifts hidden under the pews. Some have the gift of encouragement, but are not encouraging anybody. Some have the gift of teaching, but are not teaching anybody. Many have the gift of administration, but are not organizing anybody. Some have the gift of leadership, but are not leading anybody. Some have the gift of evangelism, but are not sharing the love of God and the gospel of Jesus Christ with a lost and dying world.

Growing up to the Head in His love means sharing in love. God watches what we do with what we have. Jesus told Peter to feed His sheep despite Peter not having the kind of love He asked about (John 21:17).

Journal It: Continuing the Growth

How are you using or have you used your spiritual gift(s) to build up yourself, your family, your church and your community?

_____

_____

_____

_____

_____

_____

_____

_____

_____

_____

_____

_____

_____

_____

_____

_____

_____

_____

_____

_____

_____

_____

_____

Week 4 ◆ Day 4

Spiritual Truth:

You should look like Jesus.

Memory Verse:

"And that ye put on the new man, which after God is created in righteousness and true holiness" (Ephesians 4:24).

Reading Reference:

"This I say therefore, and testify in the Lord, that ye henceforth walk not as other Gentiles walk in the vanity of their mind. Having the understanding darkened, being alienated from the life of God through the ignorance that is in them, because of the blindness of their heart: Who being past feeling have given themselves over unto lasciviousness, to work all uncleanness with greediness. But ye have not so learned Christ; If so be that ye have heard him, and have been taught by him, as the truth is in Jesus: That ye put off concerning the former conversation the old man, which is corrupt according to the deceitful lusts; And be renewed in the spirit of your mind; And that ye put on the new man, which after God is created in righteousness and true holiness" (Ephesians 4:17–24).

Who Do People Say You Look Like?

Most of us throughout our childhood are asked who do we look like, and usually we respond by naming a relative or famous person. But now that we are saved, the question we should ask ourselves is: Do I look like Jesus?

As believers, it is important that we strive to grow toward the likeness of Jesus Christ. In Ephesians 4:17–24, Paul challenged the church not to live as the unsaved, giving in to the lust of the flesh and the darkness of the world, but to be renewed in the Spirit, putting on the new man, which is after righteousness and holiness.

Growing up in His likeness means studying the habits of our Lord through His Word. You have to know Him to be like Him. The Bible is God's diary, but instead of Him keeping it a secret, He has opened it and allowed all the world to read it. Why? Because the Bible is in His likeness. The Bible holds the Word of God and God is the Word.

We can never walk in Jesus' exact steps, but we should never stop striving to fit in His shoes. Striving to walk in Jesus' shoes means measuring our every decision and evaluating all our activities against the question: What would Jesus do? We have to know Him to be like Him; therefore, we must study His Word, which tells us what He is like.

Journal It: Continuing the Growth

Stand before a full length mirror and ask yourself, "Do people tell me I look like my Heavenly Father?" Ask God to reveal to you the characteristics you have like Him and what characteristics you still have of your old father, Satan. Write down His response and pray about those characteristics that do not resemble Christ.

In order to grow up in His likeness, we must study Jesus' habits through His Word. Growing up in His likeness means measuring every decision against the question: What would Jesus do? Write down a situation you might be facing in the near future. Then, ask yourself, "What would Jesus do in this situation?" Seek your answer in His Word.

_____

_____

_____

_____

_____

_____

_____

_____

_____

_____

_____

_____

_____

_____

_____

Journal It: Continuing the Growth

_____

_____

_____

_____

_____

_____

_____

_____

_____

_____

_____

_____

_____

_____

_____

_____

_____

_____

_____

_____

_____

_____

_____

_____

_____

_____

_____

_____

_____

_____

Week 4 ◆ Day 5

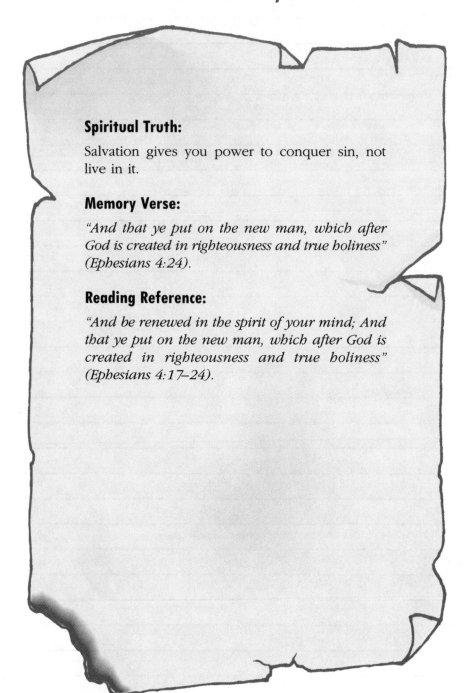

Spiritual Truth:

Salvation gives you power to conquer sin, not live in it.

Memory Verse:

"And that ye put on the new man, which after God is created in righteousness and true holiness" *(Ephesians 4:24).*

Reading Reference:

"And be renewed in the spirit of your mind; And that ye put on the new man, which after God is created in righteousness and true holiness" *(Ephesians 4:17–24).*

Life in Christ

According to Ephesians 4:23–24, when we grow up in Christ's likeness, His Word will forever be in our minds and hearts. Christ's love will be in our every action and behavior, and His power will control our selfish desires.

There are three methods by which people attempt to have a life in Christ Jesus:

- **Life of Legalism.** This is when a person thinks keeping the law can save him or her. He believes he can be saved by simply doing everything Jesus said to do perfectly. The problem is that we cannot live a sinless life. Legalism depends on goodness instead of Christ. This kind of behavior keeps a person in turmoil and eventually leads him to hell.

- **Life of License.** This is when a person thinks that he or she has a license to do anything because of grace. This cheapens God's grace. Grace does not give us a license to sin. This so-called life in Christ causes pain now and eventually leads the person who is living this way to hell.

- **Life in Christ.** The life in Christ is a life of liberty. A life of liberty gives us the power to overcome sin, but does not free us to go out and sin. Life in Christ is filled with love. A life in Christ is the only way to Christ.

Please know that you cannot have a life in Christ, if you have not accepted Christ. If your life is a life of legalism or a life of license, then there is a need for repentance and acceptance of Christ Jesus. If you believe the life of legalism or life of license best describes your life, then pray the following prayer so that you may receive Christ today and begin growing in a life in Christ.

> *Dear God, I know that Jesus is Your Son and that He died on the cross and was raised from the dead. I agree with you that I have sinned and ask forgiveness. I ask that Jesus would come into my heart as my Lord and Savior, today. I am willing to change my life and turn away from sin so that I may live a life of Christ. Thank You for forgiving me and giving me eternal life. In Jesus' name, I pray. Amen!*

After you have accepted Jesus as your Lord and Savior, join a local church right away. Pray for God to direct you to the church where He wants you to be. The local church will teach you God's principles so you can grow into a mature disciple. It will provide fellowship so you can be strengthened and encouraged by other believers. Finally, the local church is where you can join God in fulfilling His purposes.

Journal It: Continuing the Growth

Would you describe your life as a *Life of Legalism*, a *Life of License* or a *Life in Christ*? Why?

_____

_____

_____

_____

_____

_____

_____

_____

_____

_____

_____

_____

_____

_____

_____

_____

_____

_____

_____

_____

_____

_____

_____

Week 4 ◆ Day 6

Spiritual Truth:

To think right, you must keep your thoughts on Jesus.

Memory Verse

"And that ye put on the new man, which after God is created in righteousness and true holiness" (Ephesians 4:24).

Reading References:

"And be not conformed to this world: but be ye transformed by the renewing of your mind, that ye may prove what is that good, and acceptable, and perfect, will of God" (Romans 12:2).

"This I say then, Walk in the Spirit, and ye shall not fulfil the lust of the flesh" (Galatians 5:16).

"And they that are Christ's have crucified the flesh with the affections and lusts" (Galatians 5:24).

Right Thinking

We cannot live right until we think right. How do we get the right kind of thinking? There are three steps we must take to develop the right kind of thinking.

Step 1. We must be transformed by the renewing of our minds (Romans 12:2). In other words, we must change our old way of thinking to a new way of thinking in Christ Jesus. The very essence of who we are comes out of our minds so we must renew our minds.

Our minds must be renewed so we can walk in the Spirit. Before we were saved, we were mentally conscious. Our thoughts were only of worldy things because that was all that was available to us. But now that we are saved, we are spirit conscious because we can commune with the Holy Spirit. Growing up in His likeness means having the mind of Christ.

Step 2. We must treat the flesh ruthlessly (Galatians 5:24). Just as Christ crucified His flesh on Calvary's cross, so must we. To avoid sinful opportunities, we must stay out of our flesh's red light district. If we can't control our gambling, we shouldn't go to Las Vegas for vacation. If we can't control our spending, we should stay away from Neiman Marcus. Don't give the flesh any opportunity to sin.

Step 3. We must starve the flesh and feed the Spirit (Galatians 5:16). When you have a garden, you don't need to feed the weeds to make them grow. What makes the weeds grow? Nothing, they just grow. If you want your flowers or vegetables to grow, you'd better starve the weeds. Likewise, you must starve the flesh and feed the Spirit.

Don't watch violence if you have a bad temper. Don't read *Playboy* or *Playgirl,* if you toy with pornography. Cut up your credit cards, if you can't handle them. Instead, use every tool necessary to put yourself in the posture of right thinking. Read your Bible and pray every day. Go to church and Sunday School every Sunday. Assemble with other saints. Have private praise time. Listen to praise and worship music. Memorize Scriptures. Commune with God. Starve the flesh and feed the Spirit!

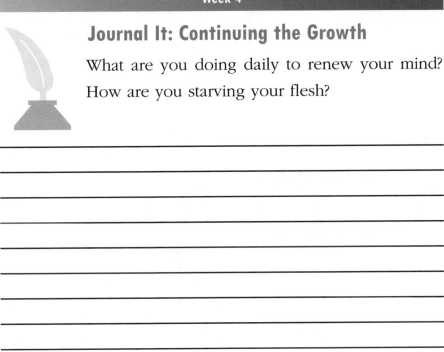

Journal It: Continuing the Growth

What are you doing daily to renew your mind?
How are you starving your flesh?

_____

_____

_____

_____

_____

_____

_____

_____

_____

_____

_____

_____

_____

_____

_____

_____

_____

_____

_____

_____

_____

_____

_____

_____

Week 4 ◆ Day 7

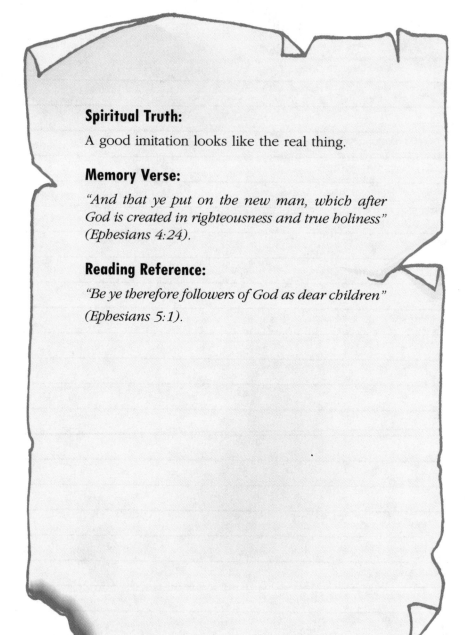

Spiritual Truth:

A good imitation looks like the real thing.

Memory Verse:

"And that ye put on the new man, which after God is created in righteousness and true holiness" *(Ephesians 4:24).*

Reading Reference:

"Be ye therefore followers of God as dear children" *(Ephesians 5:1).*

Imitators of Christ

A few years ago, ladies were spending hundreds of dollars on Louis Vuitton, Fendi and Gucci handbags. But the ladies who could not afford those $250 purses bought imitations on the street corners for about $50. Some of the imitations, or "knock-offs" as they are called, were very well made. Others could be spotted from a distance as impostors.

In the movie, *The Color Purple*, the character played by Oprah Winfrey, Sophia, recalled a day when Miss Celie, played by Whoopie Goldberg, came to her aid. Sophia explained, "When I see'd you...I know'd the'y is a God." Miss Celie had shown God's love to Sophia at a time when she could not see it on her own.

God uses us to reveal Himself to others. As Christians, when people see us, they should know there is a God because we imitate Him so well. In Ephesians 5:1, Paul encourages us to be good followers of God. We can never be God, but we can be good imitators of Him.

Imitators of Christ are knock-offs of the original. We can be well-made knock-offs or poorly-made knock-offs. We should live so that people know God exists because our love, service and giving are quality imitations of Christ.

Journal It: Continuing the Growth

Lots of people look like Jesus on Sunday; at least they think they do. But the most important thing is, and the question you should ask yourself is: Do I look like Jesus every day? As you reflect on this question, remember, looking like Jesus is much more internal then external.

_____

_____

_____

_____

_____

_____

_____

_____

_____

_____

_____

_____

_____

_____

_____

_____

_____

_____

_____

_____

_____

Reflections

What did God say to you about growing up in His love and likeness during your study this week? Record what God said, and then spend time in prayer and meditation.

_____

_____

_____

_____

_____

_____

_____

_____

_____

_____

_____

_____

_____

_____

_____

_____

_____

_____

_____

_____

_____

_____

_____

_____

_____

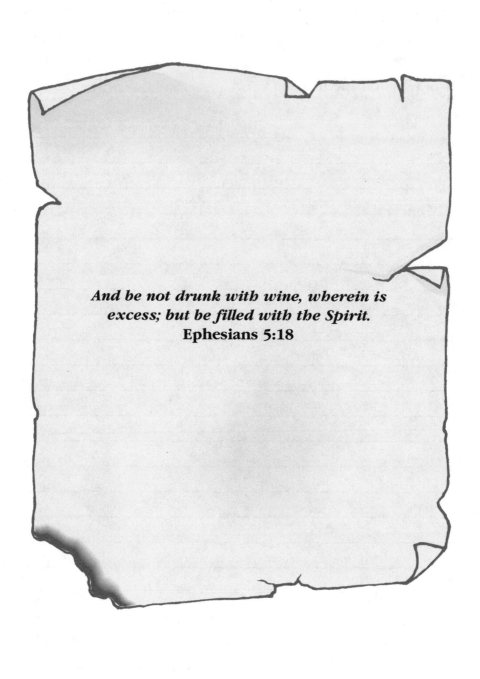

And be not drunk with wine, wherein is excess; but be filled with the Spirit.
Ephesians 5:18

Growing Up to the Head in...
His Spirit

Acknowledging God

Dear God, today I acknowledge You as God, The Holy Spirit. You are the only true and awesome triune God: God the Father, Son and Holy Ghost. I thank You, God the Father, for sitting on the throne. I thank You, God the Son, for salvation. And I thank You, God the Holy Spirit, for being here with me today. Fill me with Your Holy Spirit; not just on today, but let each and every day be a day of fresh infilling and communion with You. Let the manifestation of You, Holy Spirit, be made known in me as I do ministry, and as I live for Your kingdom building. Teach me how to grow up to the Head in You, Holy Spirit. In Your name, Lord Jesus, I give you thanks. Amen!

Week 5 ◆ Day 1

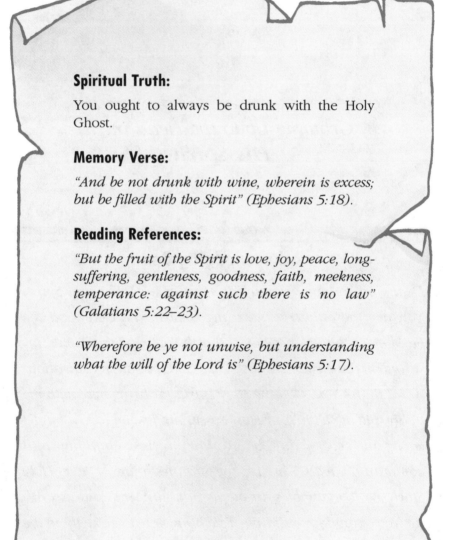

Spiritual Truth:

You ought to always be drunk with the Holy Ghost.

Memory Verse:

"And be not drunk with wine, wherein is excess; but be filled with the Spirit" (Ephesians 5:18).

Reading References:

"But the fruit of the Spirit is love, joy, peace, long-suffering, gentleness, goodness, faith, meekness, temperance: against such there is no law" (Galatians 5:22–23).

"Wherefore be ye not unwise, but understanding what the will of the Lord is" (Ephesians 5:17).

What Does It Mean to Grow Up in His Spirit?

What are some of the things we see in a drunken person? Often, a drunken person is sluggish, loud, disoriented and maybe even rude. In Ephesians 5:17–18, God tells us not to be drunk with wine, but to be filled or drunk with the Holy Spirit. If these negative traits I just mentioned are found in a drunken person, then why would God desire for us to be drunk with the Holy Spirit?

To answer this question, we must first answer the question: Why do people get drunk? People drink to fill their emptiness. They hope the drink will fill their emptiness with happiness, peace and love, but it does not. The only thing that can fill our emptiness is the Holy Spirit because the Holy Spirit is love, joy, peace—all the things we long for. God wants us to be drunk with the Spirit so He can replace our emptiness with the fruit of the Spirit (Galatians 5:22–23).

Ephesians 5:17–18 tells us that God's will is for us to be filled with His Spirit. Many of us seek only to be filled with His Word and others only with His Spirit, but there must be a balance. Those who have the Spirit without the Word will blow up, and those who have the Word without the Spirit will dry up. Those who have the Spirit and the Word will grow up.

Journal It: Continuing the Growth

Unfilled people always look for negative things to fill their emptiness, and take advantage of them. What kinds of things have you been filling yourself with? Are these things of the Spirit? If not, why? What are you willing to do to be filled with the Spirit as God desires for you?

_____

_____

_____

_____

_____

_____

_____

_____

_____

_____

_____

_____

_____

_____

_____

_____

_____

_____

_____

_____

_____

Week 5 ◆ Day 2

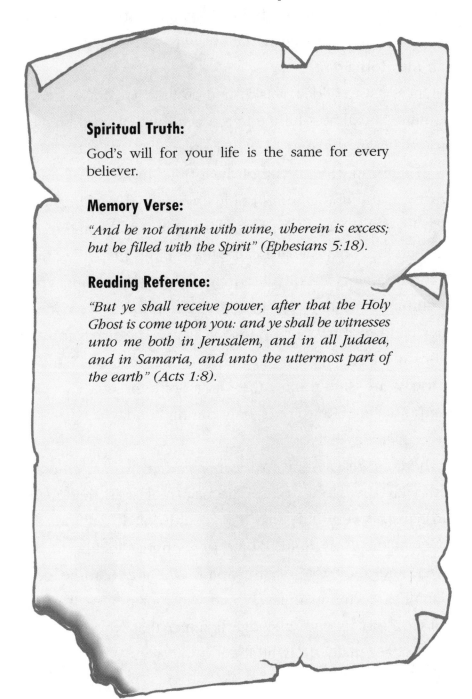

Spiritual Truth:

God's will for your life is the same for every believer.

Memory Verse:

"And be not drunk with wine, wherein is excess; but be filled with the Spirit" (Ephesians 5:18).

Reading Reference:

"But ye shall receive power, after that the Holy Ghost is come upon you: and ye shall be witnesses unto me both in Jerusalem, and in all Judaea, and in Samaria, and unto the uttermost part of the earth" (Acts 1:8).

God's Will for Every Christian

What's God's will for my life? This is a question commonly asked by many Christians. The answer is simply to be filled with the Holy Spirit.

Once, as a child, I was at church and a woman started shouting. She almost hit me in the head with her umbrella. I ducked under the pew. I asked my elders, "What's going on?" They said, "She is full of the Spirit." In my boy's mind, if that was full of the Spirit, I didn't want anything to do with it. So I spent the greater portion of my life, and some of my Christian life, doing what I call "stiff-arming" the Holy Spirit.

Stiff-arming is a football term and almost a lost art. When we stiff-arm, we have the ball in one hand, and we use the other hand to push our opponent away. The man atop the Heisman Trophy is posed in a stiff-arming position. Many of us today are stiff-arming the Holy Spirit because we are afraid of losing control; not only during Sunday service, but in our everyday lives.

There are many things we can do when we are empowered with the Holy Spirit. The sad reality is that many Christians do very little that they could not do without the power of the Holy Spirit. Some of us fight yielding to the power and direction of the Spirit. We are hard-headed, wanting to do things our way and with our power. It is not until God hits us with a sledge hammer that we say, "Well, God, I never really thought about it that way."

Growing up to the Head in His Spirit means doing things that we know for sure we could not do without the filling of the Holy Spirit. There are many things that we can do to join God in fulfilling His purposes when we are filled with the Holy Spirit; things like going to a stranger's home to talk about Jesus (Acts 1:8).

Do you know what bothers me about Christians excusing themselves from going door-to-door to witness? Jehovah Witnesses do it, and they don't believe in the power of the Holy Spirit. Yet, we who claim to believe in the power of the Holy Spirit, can't muster up enough Holy Spirit to witness door-to-door. Growing up to the Head in His Spirit means knowing there are tasks which can only be accomplished with the filling of the Holy Spirit.

Journal It: Continuing the Growth

How do you know if you are filled with the Holy Spirit? Answering this question will lead you to answer another important question: What are you doing in your Christian life that you know for sure you could not do without the filling and power of the Holy Spirit?

_____

_____

_____

_____

_____

_____

_____

_____

_____

_____

_____

_____

_____

_____

_____

_____

_____

_____

_____

_____

_____

Week 5 ◆ Day 3

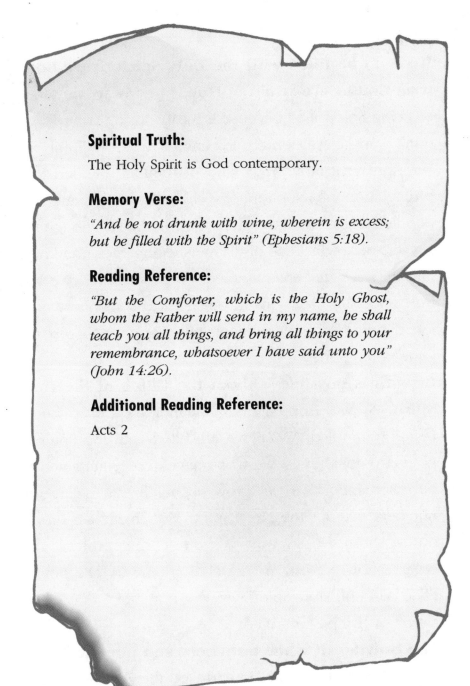

Spiritual Truth:

The Holy Spirit is God contemporary.

Memory Verse:

"And be not drunk with wine, wherein is excess; but be filled with the Spirit" (Ephesians 5:18).

Reading Reference:

"But the Comforter, which is the Holy Ghost, whom the Father will send in my name, he shall teach you all things, and bring all things to your remembrance, whatsoever I have said unto you" (John 14:26).

Additional Reading Reference:

Acts 2

Four Realities of Being Spirit-Filled

There are four realities that must be faced by anyone striving to be Spirit-filled:

1. **We can't be filled with the Holy Spirit, if we don't trust God or are afraid of Him.** Many of us are afraid of being Spirit-filled because it means losing control. We don't want to wait on the leading of the Holy Spirit. We want answers now. That kind of thinking has led to a proliferation of telephone psychics. It amazes me that people are not afraid to call psychic hotlines although the psychic networks issue disclaimers letting everyone know that they are "for entertainment purposes only." We will trust important decisions in our lives to someone whose job is primarily entertainment, but we will not trust the Omnipotent One.

2. **Growth is possible without the filling of the Holy Spirit.** Growth in numbers is no indication of a church being Spirit-filled. When we are filled with the Spirit, it pours from within us; we won't have to be entertained or be entertainers. We can grow a church that is large in numbers without the Holy Spirit. With methods, procedures, job descriptions, well-defined roles and organization, we can grow a church ministry and not be filled with the Holy Spirit. Growth in numbers is no indication of being Spirit-filled.

3. **The Holy Spirit is the only here and now God.** God the Father is on the throne and God the Son is sitting at

His right hand. The Holy Spirit is God contemporary (John 14:26). The Holy Spirit is the only real God that's here with us. He's the only on-site God. The Holy Spirit is God existential.

4. **It's God's will that we be filled.** Being filled is a duty of the believer. If we are not Spirit-filled, then we are in a backsliding posture.

Journal It: Continuing the Growth

Read Acts 2. What are some evidences of the people being filled with the Holy Spirit? What was required of the group prior to their being filled? What was the ultimate result of their being filled?

_____

_____

_____

_____

_____

_____

_____

_____

_____

_____

_____

_____

_____

_____

_____

_____

_____

_____

_____

_____

_____

_____

Week 5 ◆ Day 4

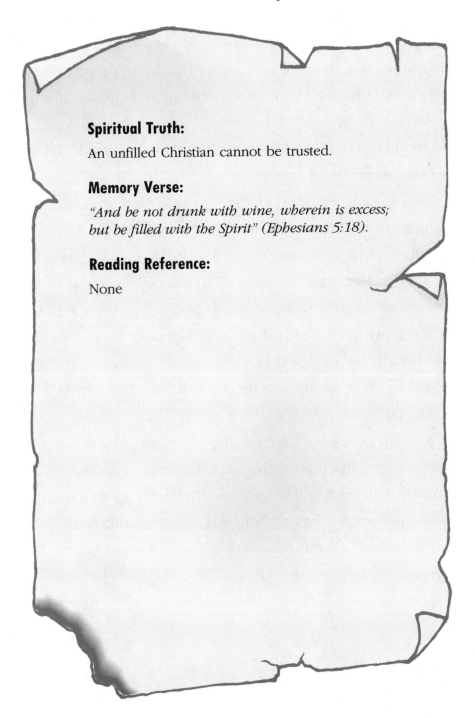

Spiritual Truth:

An unfilled Christian cannot be trusted.

Memory Verse:

"And be not drunk with wine, wherein is excess; but be filled with the Spirit" (Ephesians 5:18).

Reading Reference:

None

Manifestation of the Spirit-Filled Life

Everybody has an opinion about how believers ought to act when they are filled with the Holy Spirit. The *how* is not the most important thing; it's the filling. It doesn't matter if we shout it out or if we sit in the silence of a quiet moment. Any manifestation of how it happens is secondary to living a victorious, Spirit-filled life that abides in the Word of God and communes with Him daily.

We can't trust a person who is drunk, and we can't trust a Christian who is not filled with the Holy Spirit. Notice in Ephesians 5:18 that God puts the drunk and the unfilled Christian in the same category. Why? Because we can't trust an unfilled preacher any more than we can trust a drunk preacher. We can't trust unfilled preachers because they can only preach out of personal opinion, philosophy and experience. Unfilled preachers are no better because they, too, are talking about things that are not of God.

We can't trust unfulfilled members because they can support the church for ten years, but after one misunderstanding, will trash it like garbage. Growing up to the Head in His Spirit means remembering the best and forgetting the rest. It also means meeting biblical qualifications for leadership positions.

Journal It: Continuing the Growth

Are you a believer who can be trusted? How do you know? Are you sure that you are Spirit-filled? How do you know?

_____

_____

_____

_____

_____

_____

_____

_____

_____

_____

_____

_____

_____

_____

_____

_____

_____

_____

_____

_____

_____

_____

_____

Week 5 ◆ Day 5

Spiritual Truth:

Spirit-filled believers are powerful, not powerless.

Memory Verse:

And be not drunk with wine, wherein is excess; but be filled with the Spirit" (Ephesians 5:18).

Reading References:

"For he shall be great in the sight of the Lord, and shall drink neither wine nor strong drink; and he shall be filled with the Holy Ghost, even from his mother's womb" (Luke 1:15).

"And it came to pass, that, when Elisabeth heard the salutation of Mary, the babe leaped in her womb; and Elisabeth was filled with the Holy Ghost" (Luke 1:41).

"And his father Zacharias was filled with the Holy Ghost, and prophesied, saying, Blessed be the Lord God of Israel; for he hath visited and redeemed his people" (Luke 1:67–68).

Week 5 ◆ Day 5

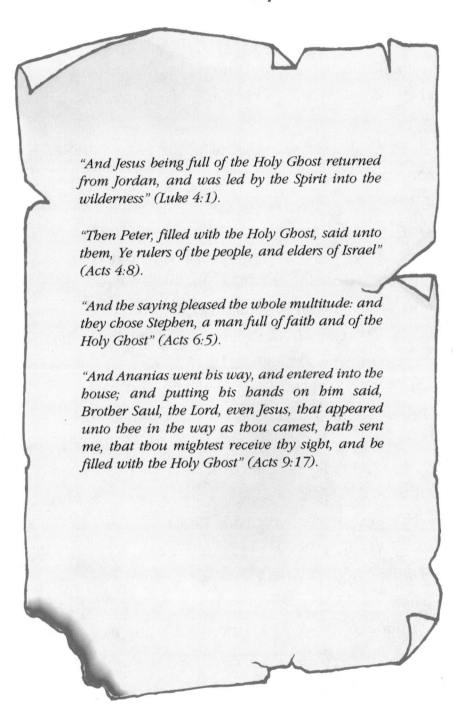

"And Jesus being full of the Holy Ghost returned from Jordan, and was led by the Spirit into the wilderness" (Luke 4:1).

"Then Peter, filled with the Holy Ghost, said unto them, Ye rulers of the people, and elders of Israel" (Acts 4:8).

"And the saying pleased the whole multitude: and they chose Stephen, a man full of faith and of the Holy Ghost" (Acts 6:5).

"And Ananias went his way, and entered into the house; and putting his hands on him said, Brother Saul, the Lord, even Jesus, that appeared unto thee in the way as thou camest, hath sent me, that thou mightest receive thy sight, and be filled with the Holy Ghost" (Acts 9:17).

Biblical Models of Being Spirit-Filled

Being filled with the Holy Spirt means being consumed by God's presence. When the Holy Spirit fills us, He empowers us to fulfill God's purposes. The Bible gives us many models of believers who were full of the Spirit and accomplished great things for God.

John the Baptist was filled with the Holy Spirit, even in his mother's womb (Luke 1:15). Luke 1:41 says his mother, Elizabeth, was also filled with the Spirit. His daddy, Zacharias, stiff-armed the Holy Spirit so God made him mute, although he held a high position in the temple. Zacharias is an example of how people can serve the Lord, yet not be filled with the Spirit. But God is a God of second chances. In verse 67, Zacharias was filled with the Holy Spirit! God opened his mouth, and he blessed the name of the Lord.

Peter was filled with the Spirit (Acts 4:8) and boldly testified about Jesus Christ. Stephen was filled with the Spirit (Acts 6:5) and did great miracles among the people. Paul was filled with the Spirit (Acts 9:17) and spread the gospel of Jesus Christ instead of crucifying Christians. Jesus was full of the Spirit (Luke 4:1) and the Spirit led Him into the wilderness where He had victory over Satan (Luke 4:13).

These biblical models show us how God can achieve much through us when we are filled with His Holy Spirit. Growing up in His Spirit means knowing that we constantly need God's power.

Journal It: Continuing the Growth

God started the church with a rushing wind and a fire. He didn't mean for it to end in a fizzle. Is that same rushing wind and fire alive in your life today? If not, what can you do to stir up the Spirit inside you?

_____

_____

_____

_____

_____

_____

_____

_____

_____

_____

_____

_____

_____

_____

_____

_____

_____

_____

_____

Week 5 ◆ Day 6

Spiritual Truth:

Spirit-filled believers make Spirit-filled churches.

Memory Verse:

"And be not drunk with wine, wherein is excess; but be filled with the Spirit" (Ephesians 5:18).

Reading Reference:

"Speaking to yourselves in psalms and hymns and spiritual songs, singing and making melody in your heart to the Lord; Giving thanks always for all things unto God and the Father in the name of our Lord Jesus Christ; Submitting yourselves one to another in the fear of God" (Ephesians 5:19–21).

Growing Up in His Spirit Is About Building Up God's Kingdom

Growing up in His Spirit means that those who are leading ministries will have received the anointing to minister. Spirit-filled believers and churches will spend their time trying to discern how to lift people up, not tear them down.

When we grow up to the Head in His Spirit, we will bring others into the kingdom and grow them up as well. A Spirit-filled person (and church) does not have room for sin, but will always make room for those who are also seeking to be filled with His Spirit.

Christians and churches that under-utilize the Holy Spirit cannot grow. You simply cannot grow beyond yourself without growing up in His Spirit. If you want to live a victorious life, you must grow up in His Spirit. If you want to help grow God's kingdom, you have to grow up in His Spirit.

It is God's will that you be filled. Growing Up to the Head in His Spirit means learning to cooperate with the Holy Spirit. We cooperate with His Spirit by:

- having a joyful relationship with Him and each other (Ephesians 5:19).
- giving thanks to the Lord (Ephesians 5:20).
- submitting to each other (Ephesians 5:21).

Journal It: Continuing the Growth

The church was born out of individuals being filled with the Spirit of God. Has your church moved away from the very "person" who gave birth to her? Have you? What can you do to embrace the Holy Spirit and build God's kingdom?

Week 5 ◆ Day 7

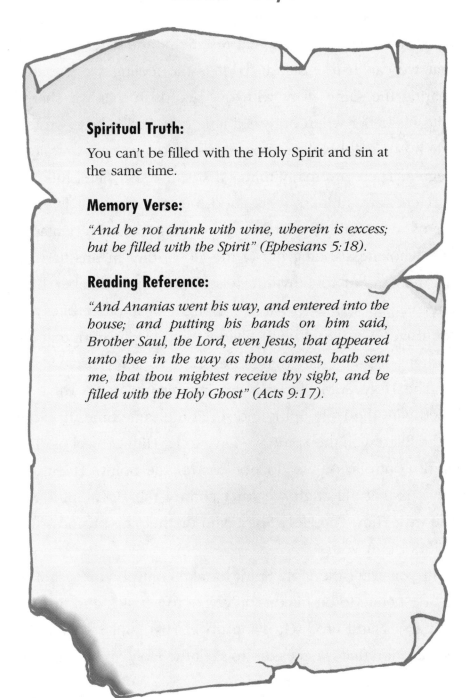

Spiritual Truth:

You can't be filled with the Holy Spirit and sin at the same time.

Memory Verse:

"And be not drunk with wine, wherein is excess; but be filled with the Spirit" (Ephesians 5:18).

Reading Reference:

"And Ananias went his way, and entered into the house; and putting his hands on him said, Brother Saul, the Lord, even Jesus, that appeared unto thee in the way as thou camest, hath sent me, that thou mightest receive thy sight, and be filled with the Holy Ghost" (Acts 9:17).

Feeling Full

What is it like to be full? Being full is like when we've gone to our favorite all-you-can-eat restaurant and eaten so much that we can hardly stand up. It is the feeling we get after sharing the same story with our grandson that we shared with his father when he was a little boy. Full is how we feel when our child walks across the stage to receive a college degree. There are many things that cause us to feel full.

Generally, fullness feels good, but sometimes it is good for us to be full of guilt because it can lead to repentance and wholeness. Being full of the Holy Spirit means there is no more room for anything else. Do you remember how after eating so much that the thought of another bite was repulsive? We should be so filled with the Holy Spirit that the thought of putting anything else inside us is repulsive.

The Holy Spirit and sin are incompatible. We can't be filled with the Holy Spirit and sin at the same time. In order to be filled with the Spirit, we have to let Him control us. The Spirit controls us; we do not control the Spirit. The good news is that although we can't control the Holy Spirit, we can trust Him. The Holy Spirit is in the helping business. He will not hurt you.

If you want the Holy Spirit to take control, you've got to get desperate to be filled. You've got to get sick and tired of being sick and tired. Growing up in His Spirit requires the desperation that is necessary to seek the Holy Spirit. It means letting the Spirit take control.

Journal It: Continuing the Growth

As you attend worship this week, remember to go Spirit-filled, and don't forget when you leave, to stay Spirit-filled. Being filled is a continuous act. You must ask God to refill you because of daily leakage.

The Holy Spirit will not only refill us, but He will also empower us to break the cycle of habitual sin that robs us and causes our vessels to leak. What things are causing constant leaks in your vessel? Pray and seek the wisdom, guidance and filling of the Holy Spirit. Ask God to reveal and remove the leaks in your life.

_____

_____

_____

_____

_____

_____

_____

_____

_____

_____

_____

_____

_____

_____

_____

_____

Journal It: Continuing the Growth

Reflections

What did God say to you this week about growing up in His Spirit? Record what God said, and then spend time in prayer and meditation.

_____

_____

_____

_____

_____

_____

_____

_____

_____

_____

_____

_____

_____

_____

_____

_____

_____

_____

_____

_____

_____

_____

_____

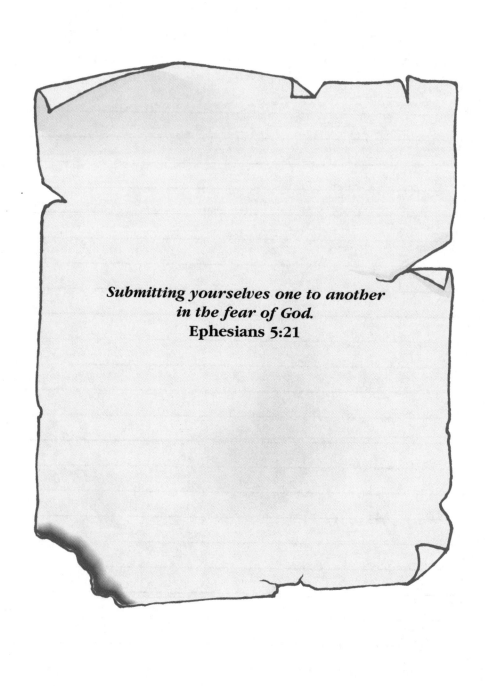

*Submitting yourselves one to another
in the fear of God.*
Ephesians 5:21

Week 6

Growing Up to the Head in...
Relationships

Acknowledging God

Dear God, today I acknowledge You as creator of all things, even relationships. May my family and I model the vertical and horizontal relationships You desire for the body of Christ. Help me to grow up in relationships with others on my job. Give me a desire to work in the workplace as though I were working for You. Place a desire within me to be concerned about and involved with the health and stability of my family and others. I pray that the love of Christ will sustain me and abide in me in all relationships, especially the one I have with You. Teach me how to grow up to the Head in relationships. In Your name, Lord Jesus, I give you thanks. Amen!

Week 6 ◆ Day 1

Spiritual Truth:

You have a responsibility to establish a relationship with God and man.

Memory Verse:

"Submitting yourselves one to another in the fear of God" (Ephesians 5:21).

Reading Reference:

"Master, which is the great commandment in the law? Jesus said unto him, Thou shalt love the Lord thy God with all thy heart, and with all thy soul, and with all thy mind. This is the first and great commandment. And the second is like unto it, Thou shalt love thy neighbour as thyself. On these two commandments hang all the law and the prophets" (Matthew 22:36–40).

What Does It Mean to Grow Up in Relationships?

Jesus clearly stated in Matthew 22:36–40 that relationship is the essential principle to individual, spiritual and church growth. Jesus was saying that these two commandments are about relationships—our relationship to God and our relationship to others. We have a responsibility to establish a relationship with God and man.

Christian relationships are similar to the horizontal and vertical directions of the cross. The vertical relationship is between us and God. The horizontal relationship is between us and humankind. Growing up to the Head in relationships means being in vertical and horizontal relationships.

In the *Antioch Effect* (Broadman & Holman, 1994), Dr. Ken Hemphill lists six necessary relationships relative to spiritual and church growth:

- **Pastor and God:** If the pastor doesn't have a relationship with God, the church is in a hurting situation.
- **Members and God:** Members should have a relationship with God.
- **Pastor and Members:** Pastors should do all they can to mend relationships with members.
- **Members and Pastor:** Members should not fight, but pray for their pastor.
- **Members and Members:** Members should not dislike, but love each other.
- **Church and Community:** The church should be active with the community and missions.

Journal It: Continuing the Growth

In order for relationships to be healthy, there must be a balance between our horizontal and vertical relationships. Examine your relationship with God and your personal relationships. Reflect on any relationship(s) that is not in balance. What personal actions will you take to grow up to the Head in these relationships?

_____

_____

_____

_____

_____

_____

_____

_____

_____

_____

_____

_____

_____

_____

_____

_____

_____

_____

_____

_____

Week 6 ◆ Day 2

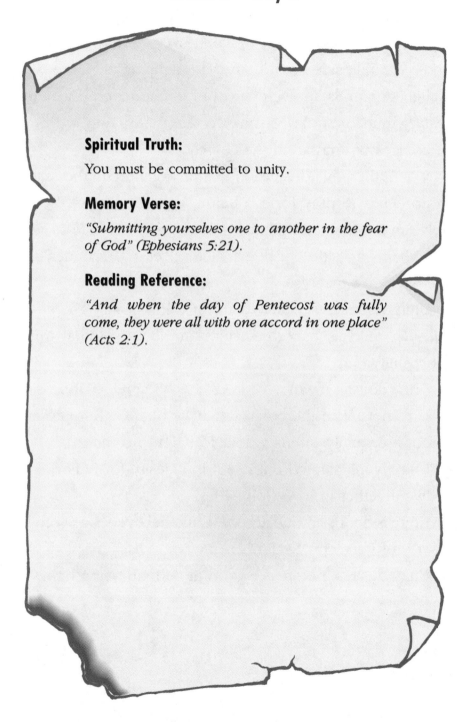

Spiritual Truth:

You must be committed to unity.

Memory Verse:

"Submitting yourselves one to another in the fear of God" (Ephesians 5:21).

Reading Reference:

"And when the day of Pentecost was fully come, they were all with one accord in one place" (Acts 2:1).

Unity

Growing up in relationships means growing up in unity. When a church is in disagreement, every group thinks that God is on their side because they are right and the other side is aligned with Satan. Differences of opinion are normal and healthy, but for some reason, we feel there is no room for differences of opinion in the church.

When there is dissension within a church, the entire group needs to pray for a solution, which is guided by the Holy Spirit. Often, everybody wants his or her side to win, but when one side considers themselves the "winner," no one wins in actuality.

Unity represents who we are in Christ Jesus. Therefore, Christian unity is expected. Here are some spiritual truths about unity:

- Unity doesn't mean everybody always agrees. Dissension does not mean there is no unity or that Satan is present, but it certainly opens a door for Him to come in.
- Unity is maintained out of Christ's desire for believers to live together in love (John 13:34–35).
- Unity is being on one accord as the believers were on the Day of Pentecost (Acts 2:2).
- Unity desires the greater good more than being right.

Journal It: Continuing the Growth

Have you ever stopped speaking to someone because they didn't think as you thought? How did you resolve it? Were you Christ-like? How has this lesson affected the way you will handle disagreements?

_____

_____

_____

_____

_____

_____

_____

_____

_____

_____

_____

_____

_____

_____

_____

_____

_____

_____

_____

_____

_____

_____

Week 6 ◆ Day 3

Spiritual Truth:

Mutual submission means Christian couples should always walk in the Spirit.

Memory Verse:

"Submitting yourselves one to another in the fear of God" (Ephesians 5:21).

Reading References:

"Wives, submit yourselves unto your own husbands, as unto the Lord. For the husband is the head of the wife, even as Christ is the head of the church: and he is the saviour of the body. Therefore as the church is subject unto Christ, so let the wives be to their own husbands in every thing. Husbands, love your wives, even as Christ also loved the church, and gave himself for it; That he might sanctify and cleanse it with the washing of water by the word, That he might present it to himself a glorious church, not having spot, or wrinkle, or any such thing; but that it should be holy and without blemish. So ought men to love their wives as their own bodies. He that loveth his wife loveth himself. For no man ever yet hated his own flesh; but nourisheth and cherisheth it, even as the Lord the church:

Week 6 ◆ Day 3

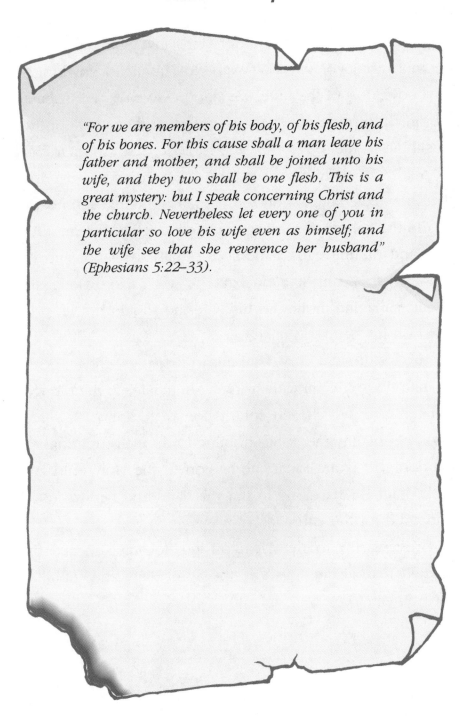

"For we are members of his body, of his flesh, and of his bones. For this cause shall a man leave his father and mother, and shall be joined unto his wife, and they two shall be one flesh. This is a great mystery: but I speak concerning Christ and the church. Nevertheless let every one of you in particular so love his wife even as himself; and the wife see that she reverence her husband" (Ephesians 5:22–33).

Growing Up in Marriage Relationships

Ephesians 5:22–33 deals primarily with the marriage relationship. Verse 21 tells us to honor Christ by submitting to one another. Some of us don't want to submit to anything or anybody. Most of the time, we skip pass verse 21. Husbands are quick to point out to their wives that they are supposed to submit to them. After all, the Bible says so. In their haste to point out their wives' failure, husbands often overlook that they have fallen short in the area of mutual submission.

Mutual submission means acknowledging one another's gifts and putting egos aside so the marital relationship can grow. That means if a husband is not as knowledgeable about managing money as his wife, he should not let pride insist on his being "in charge."

Verse 22 tells wives to submit to their husbands. Today's woman doesn't want to hear that. She chafes at the thought. But this is a self-chosen submission that cannot be forced upon her by anyone. It has nothing to do with superiority or inferiority. It is an equal submission to the Holy Spirit and each other for harmony in the marriage and family, just as Christ did for the church.

Growing up to the Head in relationships means that married people must walk in the Spirit daily and submit to each other.

Journal It: Continuing the Growth

Read Ephesians 5:21–33. What does it mean to submit one to another? Who is the husband's model of submission? Who is the wife's model of submission? How can a husband and wife better understand their relationship with each other? Why is a Spirit-filled life necessary to maintain unity in the marriage?

_____
_____
_____
_____
_____
_____
_____
_____
_____
_____
_____
_____
_____
_____
_____
_____
_____
_____
_____

Week 6 ◆ Day 4

Spiritual Truth:

It is important that your primary family be unified before trying to unify God's family.

Memory Verse:

"Submitting yourselves one to another in the fear of God" (Ephesians 5:21).

Reading Reference:

"Children, obey your parents in the Lord: for this is right. Honour thy father and mother; which is the first commandment with promise; That it may be well with thee, and thou mayest live long on the earth. And, ye fathers, provoke not your children to wrath: but bring them up in the nurture and admonition of the Lord" (Ephesians 6:1–4).

Growing Up in Family Relationships

A pastor once told me about an argument he had with his wife. As he left her sitting in their bedroom crying, he yelled, "I've got to get to church. I don't have time to fool with what you're talking about!" As he drove to the church, he realized that he could not attempt to minister to his congregation while his wife was home in tears. Realizing this, he turned the car around and headed home. He acknowledged his first responsibility as a husband. He realized that he could not be loving toward his congregation, if he failed to be loving toward his wife.

Ephesians 6:1–4 deals with the obligations of parents and children to maintain family harmony. Children are to obey their parents, and parents are to carry themselves in a manner worthy of being obeyed.

Family relationships are crucial to our growing up to the Head. How can a preacher share God's Word from the pulpit, yet ignore the role of provider and caregiver in his home? How can a pastor preach to his wife when he has been unfaithful to her? How can a youth minister prepare young people for adulthood when her daughter barely speaks to her? Sadly, such relationships occur in our churches all the time. Growing up in relationships means maintaining harmony in your family through the Holy Spirit.

Journal It: Continuing the Growth

Which family member(s) has caused you to doubt your relationship with God? Which family member(s) has motivated your relationship with God? What are some key biblical principles you use to keep harmony in your home?

_____

_____

_____

_____

_____

_____

_____

_____

_____

_____

_____

_____

_____

_____

_____

_____

_____

_____

_____

_____

Week 6 ◆ Day 5

Spiritual Truth:

All relationships are important to God, including workplace relationships.

Memory Verse:

"Submitting yourselves one to another in the fear of God" (Ephesians 5:21).

Reading Reference:

"Servants, be obedient to them that are your masters according to the flesh, with fear and trembling, in singleness of your heart, as unto Christ; Not with eyeservice, as menpleasers; but as the servants of Christ, doing the will of God from the heart; With good will doing service, as to the Lord, and not to men: Knowing that whatsoever good thing any man doeth, the same shall he receive of the Lord, whether he be bond or free. And, ye masters, do the same things unto them, forbearing threatening: knowing that your Master also is in heaven; neither is there respect of person with him" (Ephesians 6:5–9).

Growing Up in Professional Relationships

Ephesians 6:5–9 emphasizes the mutuality of work relationships. Not only must subordinates yield to those in authority, but the person with authority must not abuse the privilege. People often quit jobs because they don't want to follow orders or submit to authority. Conversely, some people abuse their authority by taking an "I'm the boss so you must do what I say" attitude. God calls both bosses and subordinates to exhibit the Spirit of Christ.

You may be wondering, "What if I'm the only Christian on my job?" Working where religion is suppressed or frowned upon is a great blessing. It's the perfect place to show the love of Christ. It's easy to be loving toward those who show love and concern for us. Growing up in relationships means showing Christ's love to those who do not know of His love.

Growing up in relationships means establishing professional relationships according to God's Word. Paul said:

- Employees, yield to the authority of your employers (v.5).
- Work as though you are working for God (v.6).
- Work with a cheerful heart (v.7).
- God will reward you for doing good (v.8).
- Employers, do not abuse your authority (v.9).

Journal It: Continuing the Growth

What is your work environment like? How do you relate to people in the workplace? What about those in authority over you, even in the church? Is your response to those in authority over you Christ-like?

_____

_____

_____

_____

_____

_____

_____

_____

_____

_____

_____

_____

_____

_____

_____

_____

_____

_____

_____

_____

Week 6 ◆ Day 6

Spiritual Truth:

Churches should always look to resolve conflict.

Memory Verse:

"Submitting yourselves one to another in the fear of God" (Ephesians 5:21).

Reading References:

"Therefore if thou bring thy gift to the altar, and there rememberest that thy brother hath ought against thee; Leave there thy gift before the altar, and go thy way; first be reconciled to thy brother, and then come and offer thy gift" (Matthew 5:23–24).

"Moreover if thy brother shall trespass against thee, go and tell him his fault between thee and him alone: if he shall hear thee, thou hast gained thy brother. But if he will not hear thee, then take with thee one or two more, that in the mouth of two or three witnesses every word may be established. And if he shall neglect to hear them, tell it unto the church: but if he neglect to hear the church, let him be unto thee as an heathen man and a publican" (Matthew 18:15–17).

Relationships and Building God's Kingdom

A church growing up in relationships will become a growing church because people come to church seeking love, acceptance and understanding. Empty pews are an indictment of our own carnality. It is futile for us to try to maintain a right relationship with God through worship and giving, if we are not at peace with others.

Jesus gives us two models for handling conflict in our relationships. In Matthew 5:23–24, He tells us that when we are at odds with someone, we should attempt reconciliation before offering a gift to God. God gets greater joy and glory from our gift when we have reconciled with our brother. Matthew 18:15–17 instructs us to make every attempt to restore harmony to our broken or bruised relationships. It doesn't matter who was wrong. Growing up in relationships means casting out pride so restoration can occur.

Some truths about the church and conflict are:

- How well a church manages conflict is a major determining factor in numerical growth.
- Churches whose members have immature relationships will have lingering, interminable conflict.
- Churches that have grown up to the Head in relationships will meet conflict positively with a commitment to resolution and restoration.

Journal It: Continuing the Growth

Think of a time when there was a disagreement within your church body. Did the congregation maintain unity even though there was disagreement? What actions were taken to resolve the conflict? Did the action reflect a congregation growing up to the Head in relationships? How did you respond to the situation? Was your response Christ-like?

_____

_____

_____

_____

_____

_____

_____

_____

_____

_____

_____

_____

_____

_____

_____

_____

_____

_____

_____

Week 6 ◆ Day 7

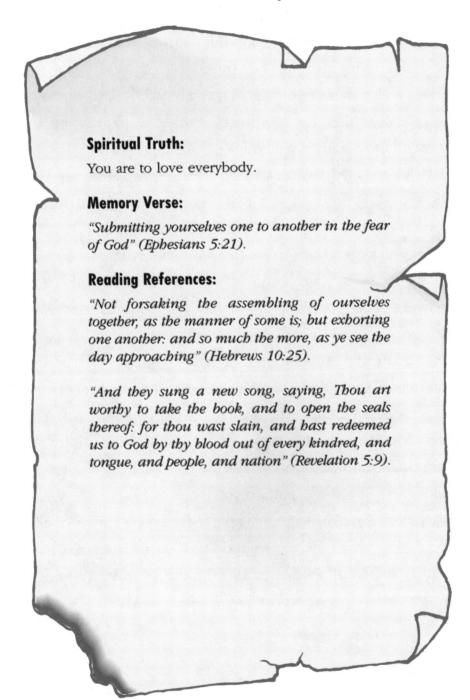

Spiritual Truth:

You are to love everybody.

Memory Verse:

"Submitting yourselves one to another in the fear of God" (Ephesians 5:21).

Reading References:

"Not forsaking the assembling of ourselves together, as the manner of some is; but exhorting one another: and so much the more, as ye see the day approaching" (Hebrews 10:25).

"And they sung a new song, saying, Thou art worthy to take the book, and to open the seals thereof: for thou wast slain, and hast redeemed us to God by thy blood out of every kindred, and tongue, and people, and nation" (Revelation 5:9).

What a Fellowship!

One of the things I've noticed is that many people fellow-ship after worship service, but only with people they already know. Growing up to the Head in relationships means getting to know new people. One day, we will all meet "in that great getting up morning," and it won't just be our friends there; neither will it be just blacks or whites. It will be an eternal fellowship with the Father, the Son, the Holy Ghost and every believer from every nation and tongue (Revelation 5:9).

Growing up to the Head in relationships means demon-strating Christ's love through our fellowship with other believers. Too often we go to church and say "hello" to everyone, but never have real fellowship. One of the ways we encourage fellowship at our church is through Fulfillment Hour. Many churches refer to it as Sunday School, but we call it Fulfillment Hour because it is more than just a class. It's where we come to share our sorrows, joys and testimonies of what God has done in our lives so we can build each other up. Fulfillment Hour is where we get to know our Christian brothers and sisters on a much deeper level than "Hi, how are you doing?" First Peter 3:8 says, *"Finally, be ye all of one mind, having compassion one of another, love as brethren, be pitiful, be courteous."*

Journal It: Continuing the Growth

What is your level of fellowship with other believers? Is it, "Hi!" and "Bye!" or does it go deeper? Why?

In our church, we sing a welcome song, walk around and greet each other in order to get to know other believers. What can you do to get to know other saints each time you come together?

_____

_____

_____

_____

_____

_____

_____

_____

_____

_____

_____

_____

_____

_____

_____

_____

_____

_____

Reflections

What did God say to you this week about growing up in relationships?

Reflections

_____

_____

_____

_____

_____

_____

_____

_____

_____

_____

_____

_____

_____

_____

_____

_____

_____

_____

_____

_____

_____

_____

_____

_____

_____

_____

_____

_____

_____

_____

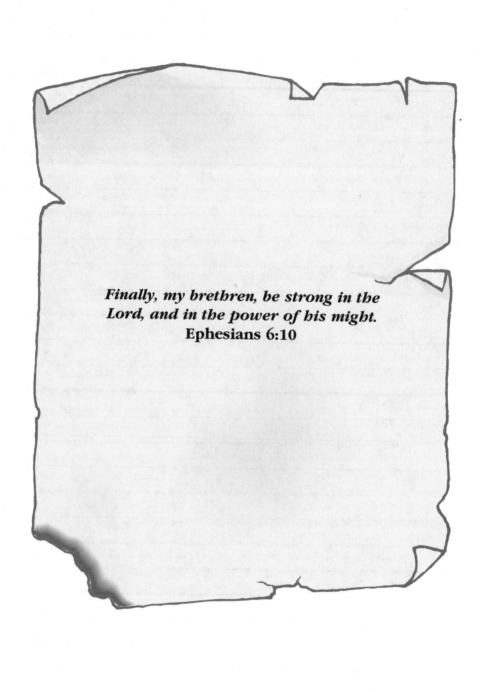

Finally, my brethren, be strong in the
Lord, and in the power of his might.
Ephesians 6:10

Growing Up to the Head in...
His Strength

Acknowledging God

Dear God, today I acknowledge You as my God of strength. I praise You for Your power and Your might. Holy Spirit, I invite You to walk with me daily, and to keep me dressed in Your armor, which is the attire I need for spiritual success. Help me to wear it well. Each day, remind me, dear Lord, to put on Your whole armor—the belt of truth, the breastplate of righteousness, shoes of preparation, the shield of faith, the helmet of salvation and the sword of the Spirit, which is Your Word. After I am dressed, help me not to forget to shine my armor with prayer. Thank You that I am in a battle that is already won. Help me to not give in to unnecessary defeat from the enemy. Finally, keep me strong in Your love and in the power of Your might. Teach me how to grow up to the Head in Your strength for the victory is already mine. Praise ye the Lord God Almighty! In Jesus name, Amen!

Week 7 ◆ Day 1

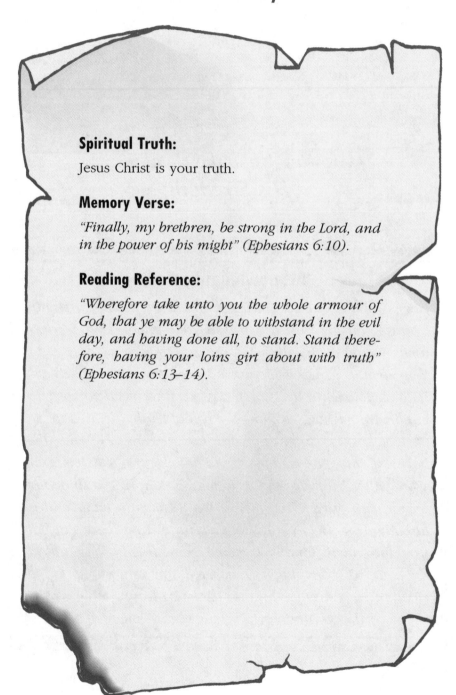

Spiritual Truth:

Jesus Christ is your truth.

Memory Verse:

"Finally, my brethren, be strong in the Lord, and in the power of his might" (Ephesians 6:10).

Reading Reference:

"Wherefore take unto you the whole armour of God, that ye may be able to withstand in the evil day, and having done all, to stand. Stand therefore, having your loins girt about with truth" (Ephesians 6:13–14).

Dress for Success

We live in a world of designer clothing that changes every year according to the latest fashions, but that's material clothing. God has designed clothing for believers—God's Designer Wear. Paul refers to it as the armor of God and tells us to put it on so we can withstand the evil in each day.

If we want to dress for spiritual success, then we need to put on God's Designer Wear. In the battle between God and Satan, God's soldiers must dress for spiritual success. Any soldier going onto the battlefield not prepared for combat will be defeated. If we do not wear God's armor, we are already defeated. It's only a matter of when we find out. Today, we will look at the first piece of spiritual armor, the belt of truth.

The Belt of Truth

In Ephesians 6:13–14a, Paul instructs us to put on the belt of truth. What is this belt of truth? Christ is the belt that we must wear. The gospel of Jesus Christ is our doctrine of truth. Knowing the truth of who Christ is keeps us from flapping from one false doctrine to another. The belt of truth gives us strength and support in times of trial and tribulation. It helps us walk with confidence and security.

Journal It: Continuing the Growth

The primary purpose of a belt is to hold up our pants and keep our shirts tucked in. A soldier who is caught with his pants down can get into a lot of trouble. What about an unstable Christian? Place a belt around your waist. Think of it as a soldier's belt. What relationship do you see between a soldier's belt and the belt of truth?

_____

_____

_____

_____

_____

_____

_____

_____

_____

_____

_____

_____

_____

_____

_____

_____

_____

_____

_____

Week 7 ◆ Day 2

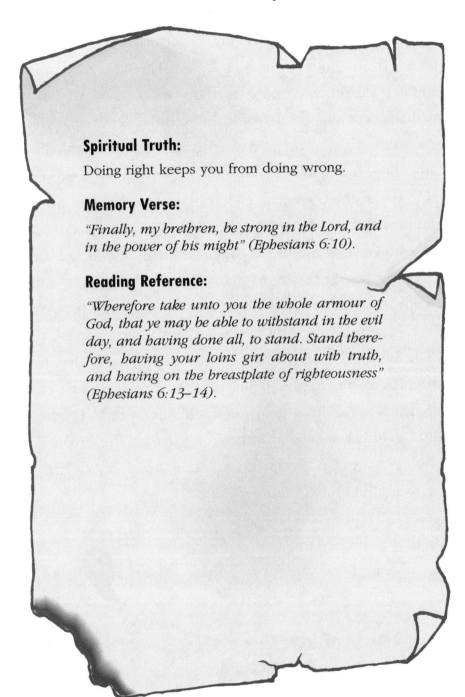

Spiritual Truth:

Doing right keeps you from doing wrong.

Memory Verse:

"Finally, my brethren, be strong in the Lord, and in the power of his might" (Ephesians 6:10).

Reading Reference:

"Wherefore take unto you the whole armour of God, that ye may be able to withstand in the evil day, and having done all, to stand. Stand therefore, having your loins girt about with truth, and having on the breastplate of righteousness" (Ephesians 6:13–14).

Breastplate of Righteousness

The accessories make the difference in our clothing. You can have on a nice suit, but if the tie, shirt or shoes are not coordinated, the beauty of the suit is lost. Likewise, the proper spiritual accessories prepare us to do God's work. We can be Christians, yet still be defeated in spiritual warfare because we are not wearing the accessories we need for battle.

In Ephesians 6:13–14, Paul tells us to put on the breastplate of righteousness. What is this breastplate of righteousness we should be wearing? We have been made right with God by the blood of Jesus Christ. Still as believers, we have a responsibility to live right. We have been called to walk in righteousness; therefore, we must not give in to doing wrong. Doing right keeps us from doing wrong.

The breastplate of righteousness covers our bodies from our necks to our thighs. It protects the internal parts; especially the soul and the heart. It shields us from losing heart. It also shields our hearts from wrong living. The breastplate of righteousness protects the spiritual heart of a Christian from being fatally wounded in battle.

Journal It: Continuing the Growth

Take a large towel and pin it in front of you. Think of it as a soldier's breastplate. How does the soldier's breastplate relate to the breastplate of righteousness? What could happen to believers who do not wear their breastplates? What things in your life do you need the breastplate of righteousness to protect you from?

_____

_____

_____

_____

_____

_____

_____

_____

_____

_____

_____

_____

_____

_____

_____

_____

_____

_____

_____

Week 7 ◆ Day 3

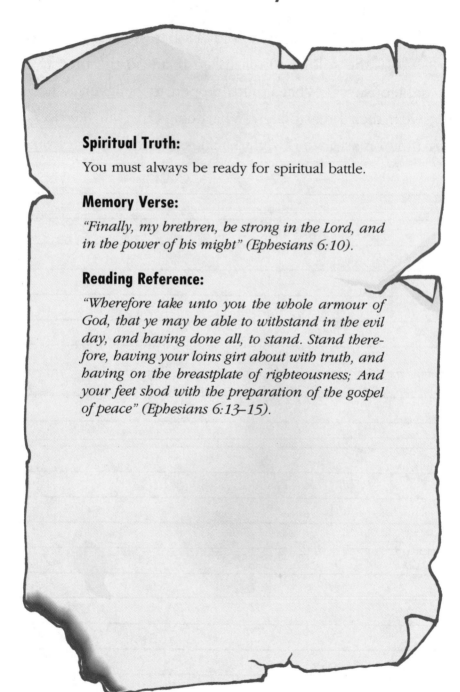

Spiritual Truth:

You must always be ready for spiritual battle.

Memory Verse:

"Finally, my brethren, be strong in the Lord, and in the power of his might" (Ephesians 6:10).

Reading Reference:

"Wherefore take unto you the whole armour of God, that ye may be able to withstand in the evil day, and having done all, to stand. Stand therefore, having your loins girt about with truth, and having on the breastplate of righteousness; And your feet shod with the preparation of the gospel of peace" (Ephesians 6:13–15).

Shoes of Preparation

The third article that God gives us is sandals, which are the gospel of peace. Shoes are a sign of readiness. If your family is getting ready to leave the house to go to church, and all of a sudden somebody announces she can't find her shoes, it means that person isn't ready to go. We are not ready to go anywhere until we put on our shoes. The Gospel tells us that we should not dare go to war without our shoes.

There is a difference between shoes for dancing and shoes for battle. Dancing shoes are slick on the bottom. When we are going to battle, we need some grip, something to give us some leverage. We need to put on soldier's shoes with cleats or grips. David calls them hinds (deer) feet in Psalm 18:33. Hinds feet defy gravity so God can sit us in high places where Satan can do us no harm.

In Ephesians 6:15, Paul tells us to put on the shoes of preparation. The Christian's shoes of preparation represent readiness for spiritual battle. Satan is always ready for battle. In fact, he always starts the war. Therefore, we must be ready for the attack that we know is coming. We should always be dressed in our spiritual shoes because we never know when we will be led by the Holy Spirit to share the gospel of peace.

Journal It: Continuing the Growth

Shoes cover and protect our feet. Usually when we get ready to go somewhere the last thing we put on is our shoes. Put on a pair of shoes and imagine them to be the shoes of a soldier. How do soldiers' shoes relate to the shoes of preparation Christians are to wear? What are some spiritual warfare conditions or situations that you must be ready to walk through?

_____
_____
_____
_____
_____
_____
_____
_____
_____
_____
_____
_____
_____
_____
_____
_____
_____
_____
_____
_____

Week 7 ◆ Day 4

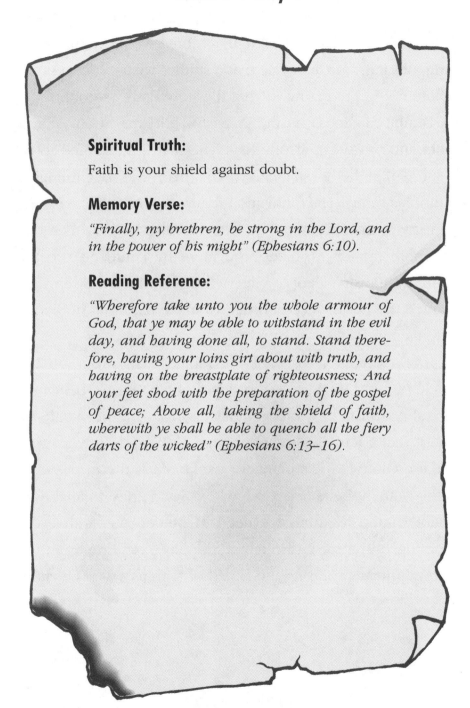

Spiritual Truth:

Faith is your shield against doubt.

Memory Verse:

"Finally, my brethren, be strong in the Lord, and in the power of his might" (Ephesians 6:10).

Reading Reference:

"Wherefore take unto you the whole armour of God, that ye may be able to withstand in the evil day, and having done all, to stand. Stand therefore, having your loins girt about with truth, and having on the breastplate of righteousness; And your feet shod with the preparation of the gospel of peace; Above all, taking the shield of faith, wherewith ye shall be able to quench all the fiery darts of the wicked" (Ephesians 6:13–16).

Shield of Faith

The shield of faith is our fourth article of spiritual clothing. This shield is not a small shield, as some would think. It is a long, oblong, sturdy device that a soldier wears. It covers the whole body, protecting it from the fiery darts of doubt.

Doubt can mess us up. A pastor told me about a man who came to see him one day. The man just wanted to be assured that he wasn't crazy. The man was beginning to doubt his sanity. His motivation for work was to increase the ministry of the church, so he worked hard. He reasoned that the more money he made, the more he could give to the church's ministry. People were telling him he was crazy. He wanted the pastor to pinch him to make sure that he hadn't lost his mind.

In Ephesians 6:16, Paul encourages us to put on the shield of faith. What does the shield of faith do for believers? The shield of faith protects believers from the fiery darts of doubt that Satan is shooting at us. Satan uses adversity to make us doubt God's plans for us. Doubt is the opposite of faith. Faith is believing God when Satan tries to make us doubt Him. Therefore, we need to put on our faith every morning, and wear it throughout the day. Growing up in His strength means wearing the shield of faith as our protection.

Journal It: Continuing the Growth

The shield covers a soldier's entire body protecting it from fiery darts being shot at him. Hold a large lid in front of you (like a trash can lid). Imagine you're holding a soldier's shield. How does it relate to the shield of faith we should be wearing?

_____

_____

_____

_____

_____

_____

_____

_____

_____

_____

_____

_____

_____

_____

_____

_____

_____

_____

_____

_____

Week 7 ◆ Day 5

Spiritual Truth:

Salvation transforms your mind so you no longer rely on human reason, but on faith.

Memory Verse:

"Finally, my brethren, be strong in the Lord, and in the power of his might" (Ephesians 6:10).

Reading Reference:

"Wherefore take unto you the whole armour of God, that ye may be able to withstand in the evil day, and having done all, to stand. Stand therefore, having your loins girt about with truth, and having on the breastplate of righteousness; And your feet shod with the preparation of the gospel of peace; Above all, taking the shield of faith, wherewith ye shall be able to quench all the fiery darts of the wicked. And take the helmet of salvation" (Ephesians 6:13–17).

Additional Reading Reference:

Mark 5:1–15

Helmet of Salvation

Jesus healed a lunatic, a man called Legion, who was cutting himself in the graveyard (Mark 5:1–15). This man didn't even know his real name, but called himself Legion because there were so many demons inside of him. Jesus delivered the man by casting the demons into a herd of pigs. The pigs, possessed with the demons, drowned themselves in the sea.

The Bible says that when the townspeople came, the man was sitting up, clothed in his right mind. But the people did not rejoice in this man's salvation. They were upset about the pigs and told Jesus to leave.

I'm not too sure that we aren't the same today as those people were. With our love for materialism, we can shout over material things, but can't give a word of praise for God when He saves someone.

In Ephesians 6:17a, Paul encourages us to put on the fifth garment of our armor, the helmet of salvation. The helmet of salvation reminds us that we are already covered by the blood of Jesus Christ. Before salvation a person's mind could not reason correctly, but once saved, he can rely on his faith to reason and renew his mind. Growing up in His strength means having a renewed mind.

Journal It: Continuing the Growth

A soldier's helmet covers and protects his head. Place a hat upon your head, and imagine it to be a soldier's helmet. How does it relate to the helmet of salvation? Why is it important to protect your head?

_____

_____

_____

_____

_____

_____

_____

_____

_____

_____

_____

_____

_____

_____

_____

_____

_____

_____

_____

_____

Week 7 ◆ Day 6

Spiritual Truth:

God's Word is your offensive weapon in spiritual warfare.

Memory Verse:

"Finally, my brethren, be strong in the Lord, and in the power of his might" (Ephesians 6:10).

Reading Reference:

"Wherefore take unto you the whole armour of God, that ye may be able to withstand in the evil day, and having done all, to stand. Stand therefore, having your loins girt about with truth, and having on the breastplate of righteousness; And your feet shod with the preparation of the gospel of peace; Above all, taking the shield of faith, wherewith ye shall be able to quench all the fiery darts of the wicked. And take the helmet of salvation, and the sword of the Spirit, which is the word of God" (Ephesians 6:13–17).

Sword of the Spirit

The final article that completes the armor of God is the sword of the Spirit, which is the Word of God. A Christian is naked without the Word of God. Being naked is not being dressed for spiritual success.

Psalm 119:11 tells us of the importance of God's Word: *"Thy word have I hid in mine heart, that I might not sin against thee."* We need the Word in order to do spiritual battle. The Word is the only offensive weapon in God's Designer Wear. Everything else is designed for defense.

The Word is a two-edged sword. Hebrews 4:12 says:

> *For the word of God is quick, and powerful, and sharper than any two-edged sword, piercing even to the dividing asunder of soul and spirit, and of the joints and marrow, and is a discerner of the thoughts and intents of the heart.*

A double-edged sword cuts two ways. It cuts to comfort those who need comforting, but it also cuts to disturb those who need disturbing. Some people come to church in need of a word of comfort. Others come needing a word of conviction and a word of disturbance. The sword of the Spirit is a powerful weapon. It can heal the wounded and cut the enemy.

Journal It: Continuing the Growth

Pick up a stick and imagine it to be a soldier's sword. Now put it down and pick up your Bible. How does the soldier's sword relate to the sword of the Spirit, the Word of God? Why is it a double-edged sword? What would be the result of a single-edged or dull sword? Consider a spiritual battle you are currently facing. Find Scriptures to use as your weapon against Satan.

_____

_____

_____

_____

_____

_____

_____

_____

_____

_____

_____

_____

_____

_____

_____

_____

_____

_____

_____

Week 7 ◆ Day 7

Spiritual Truth:

If you want to dress for spiritual success put on God's Designer Wear—the whole armor of God.

Memory Verse:

"Finally, my brethren, be strong in the Lord, and in the power of his might" (Ephesians 6:10).

Reading Reference:

"Wherefore take unto you the whole armour of God, that ye may be able to withstand in the evil day, and having done all, to stand. Stand therefore, having your loins girt about with truth, and having on the breastplate of righteousness; And your feet shod with the preparation of the gospel of peace; Above all, taking the shield of faith, wherewith ye shall be able to quench all the fiery darts of the wicked. And take the helmet of salvation, and the sword of the Spirit, which is the word of God. Praying always with all prayer and supplication in the Spirit, and watching thereunto with all perseverance and supplication for all saints" (Ephesians 6:13–18).

The Problem of "Dressing Down"

Dressing down is popular today. In corporate America, there is "dress down" or "casual" day. It is good to relax and get comfortable. However, there is a danger when we dress down in spiritual battle.

This game of spiritual warfare is played from the cradle to the grave. A lot of teams lose in the fourth quarter or the last sixty seconds of the game. So don't dress down! Growing up in His strength means not dressing down.

The problem with dressing down is that some of us only dress in the helmet of salvation and never pick up the sword of the Spirit, the Word of God. Some of us pick up the sword, but never put on the helmet of salvation. We think we can fight Satan by carrying our Bible, but the size of a Bible will not defeat Satan. Some of us put on the shoes of preparation, but never do anything because we leave our shield of faith at home. Some of us put on the belt of truth, but not the breastplate of righteousness.

Growing up in His strength means relying on God's power, not our own. We must put on the *whole* armor of God every day. We can't afford to not put on any piece of the armor or to not wear it every day. The armor empowers us to fight Satan and live victoriously.

Journal It: Continuing the Growth

Check your armor! Periodically, every soldier's equipment must pass inspection. If Christ were looking at your armor today, what would He see? What do you believe would be His evaluation of your attire? Would He say that you have been dressing down?

_____

_____

_____

_____

_____

_____

_____

_____

_____

_____

_____

_____

_____

_____

_____

_____

_____

_____

_____

_____

Reflections

What did God say to you about growing up in His Strength during this week's study? Record what He said, and then pray for God to help you rely on His power.

_____

_____

_____

_____

_____

_____

_____

_____

_____

_____

_____

_____

_____

_____

_____

_____

_____

_____

_____

_____

_____

_____

_____

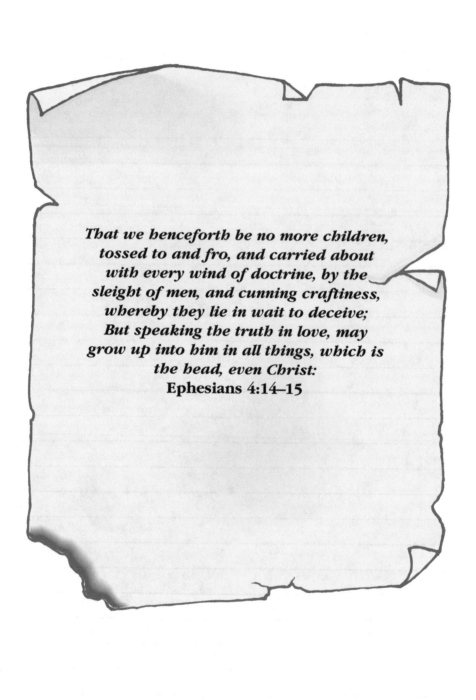

That we henceforth be no more children, tossed to and fro, and carried about with every wind of doctrine, by the sleight of men, and cunning craftiness, whereby they lie in wait to deceive; But speaking the truth in love, may grow up into him in all things, which is the head, even Christ:
Ephesians 4:14–15

End of the Journey:
Beginning of Discipleship

Acknowledging God

*Dear God, thank You for **Seven Weeks of Growing Up to the Head**. Thank You for growing me up to Your Head in your everlasting joy, grace, reconciliation, purpose, prayer, love, likeness, Spirit, relationships and strength. Thank You that this study has not only heightened my awareness about who I am in Christ, but has truly inspired me to live as a disciple of Christ. Now unto You, my Lord and Savior, Jesus Christ, who is able to do exceeding abundantly above all that I can ask or think, to You be all the glory, forevermore. Amen!*

Reflections

You have come to the end of your *Seven Weeks of Growing Up to the Head* journey, but this is not the end of your spiritual journey with God. In fact, it is just the beginning. Prayerfully, this study has inspired your quiet time with God and moved you to the next level in Christ—discipleship. Reflect on the last seven weeks. How has this study helped you grow up to the Head?

_____

_____

_____

_____

_____

_____

_____

_____

_____

_____

_____

_____

_____

_____

_____

_____

_____

_____

_____

Reflections

_____

_____

_____

_____

_____

_____

_____

_____

_____

_____

_____

_____

_____

_____

_____

_____

_____

_____

_____

_____

_____

_____

_____

_____

_____

_____

_____

_____

_____

_____

Reflections

Seven Weeks of Growing Up to the Head

Reflections

_____

_____

_____

_____

_____

_____

_____

_____

_____

_____

_____

_____

_____

_____

_____

_____

_____

_____

_____

_____

_____

_____

_____

_____

_____

_____

_____

_____

Reflections

_____

_____

_____

_____

_____

_____

_____

_____

_____

_____

_____

_____

_____

_____

_____

_____

_____

_____

_____

_____

_____

_____

_____

_____

_____

_____

_____

_____

THE AUTHOR'S COLLECTION
Committed to Doing Church God's Way

God has given me a burning passion for biblically-based kingdom building and spiritual growth. Through His Spirit, I have discerned and recorded in my books discipleship principles related to church growth, evangelism, personal spiritual development, praise and worship. I recommend the following titles to those who are serious about *doing church God's way*.

Church Growth and Kingdom Building

Faithful Over a Few Things: Seven Critical Church Growth Principles bridges the gap between theory and practice. It offers seven principles that, when faithfully implemented, will cause your church to grow. A study guide and resource kit are available. The resource kit contains a workbook, transparencies and a videotape.

Sin in the House: Ten Crucial Church Problems with Cleansing Solutions examines problems that hinder growth and offers proven solutions. This book addresses the question of why you and your church are not growing.

Fulfillment Hour: Fulfilling God's Purposes for the Church Through the Sunday School Hour by Jackie S. Henderson and Joan W. Johnson presents a nontraditional Sunday School model that fulfills all of the purposes and mission of the church through a systematic, balanced and creative approach within the context of an hour. *Fulfillment Hour* gives a detailed explanation of the concept, process and procedures of the model. The model can be applied by any denomination or church.

Evangelism

Breaking the Huddle contains twelve messages that deal with the central theme of fulfilling Jesus' purpose of seeking and saving the lost (Luke 19:10). Like a football team, the church must break the huddle; that is, leave the comfort of the sanctuary and obediently go out among the unsaved to share the Gospel.

Stewardship

Faith Raising vs. Money Raising is the most complete stewardship resource available today. It presents a biblically-based approach to doing stewardship God's way. The book describes a proven stewardship plan that can be implemented in any church and any denomination. It also provides advice on how to raise capital for building projects and includes a study guide and teaching aid.

Personal Spiritual Development

Growing Up to the Head: Ten Essentials to Becoming a Better Christian challenges the reader to mature spiritually by growing up to the fullness of Christ. The study is based on the book of Ephesians. The book uniquely relates personal spiritual growth to numerical congregational growth. The book is designed as a congregational study. A participant's guide and leader's guide are available for small group study. The new companion text, **Seven Weeks of Growing Up to the Head**, is for individual study.

Stir Up the Gifts: Empowering Believers for Victorious Living and Ministry Tasks is a complete, practical guide on spiritual gifts that is applicable for any denomination. The book is based on 2 Timothy 1:6 where Paul tells us to stir up the gift and bring the fire to a flame. Study of this book will fire you up and revolutionize the ministries in your church. A leader's guide and study guide are available.

How to Be Blessed: Finding Favor with God and Man is a biblical guide to being blessed according to God's Word. It is based on the truth that God promises to bless His obedient children. This book will protect you from finding out too late about all the blessings that were yours, but you never received.

When Black Men Stretch Their Hands to God is based on the prophecy: When black men stretch their hands to God in submission and adoration, there will be a revival in the land for all people that is unparalleled. I believe that God is calling black men to model for the world what it means to love God, themselves, their families and all mankind. Through their submission, God will use black men to bring reconciliation to all of His people.

However, reconciliation and revival must begin with knowing who we are and whose we are. This book affirms the biblical black heritage that has been ignored, misconstrued, misinterpreted and, in some cases, entirely removed. My goal is to eradicate ignorance, correct racist interpretations and affirm the existence of the rich heritage and presence of black people and people of color in the Bible.

Praise and Worship

Although the title is colorful, *Praising the Hell Out of Yourself* is a beneficial discipleship approach to praise and worship. It offers praise as an antidote for evil and provides the "how, why and when" of entering into His presence. A workbook, CD and T-shirt are available.

Inspiration

My wife's autobiography, *Tough Enough: Trials on Every Hand,* describes how God transformed a shy, reserved, country girl from Alabama into a bold, self-assured, yet humble helpmeet to her husband and spokesperson for the Lord. Truly, her testimony of faith will encourage you.

Black History

A Good Black Samaritan teaches biblical black history—specifically how Jesus used people of color to teach the world what is good.

Other Resources by George O. McCalep, Jr., Ph.D.
Committed to Doing Church God's Way

ORDER FORM

QTY	ITEM	EACH	TOTAL
	Faithful Over a Few Things	$19.95	$
	Faithful Over a Few Things—Study Guide	9.95	
	Faithful Over a Few Things—Audio Version	14.95	
	Faithful Over a Few Things—Resource Kit	189.95	
	Breaking the Huddle	14.95	
	Breaking the Huddle—Sermonic Audiocassette	10.00	
	Growing Up to the Head	19.95	
	Growing Up to the Head—Leader's Guide	10.95	
	Growing Up to the Head—Participant's Guide	10.95	
	Seven Weeks of Growing Up to the Head	19.95	
	Stir Up the Gifts	24.95	
	Stir Up the Gifts—Leader's Guide	10.95	
	Stir Up the Gifts—Workbook & Study Guide	10.95	
	Stir Up the Gifts—Sermonic Audio Series	19.95	
	Praising the Hell Out of Yourself	19.95	
	Praising the Hell Out of Yourself—Workbook	14.95	
	Praising the Hell Out of Yourself—CD	14.95	
	Praising the Hell Out of Yourself—T-Shirt (L, XL, XXL, XXXL)	10.00	
	Sin in the House	19.95	
	How to Be Blessed	19.95	
	"Jabez's Prayer"—Sermonic Audio Series	19.95	
	A Good Black Samaritan	3.95	
	Messages of Victory for God's Church in the New Millennium—Sermonic Audio Series	19.95	
	Tough Enough: Trials on Every Hand by Sadie T. McCalep, Ph.D.	20.00	
	Fulfillment Hour by Jackie S. Henderson & Joan W. Johnson, compiled and edited by George O. McCalep, Jr., Ph.D.	24.95	
	Faith Raising vs. Money Raising	24.95	
	When Black Men Stretch Their Hands to God	24.95	
	Subtotal		

Order by phone, fax, mail or online

Orman Press   www.ormanpress.com
4200 Sandy Lake Drive
Lithonia, GA 30038
Phone: 770-808-0999
Fax: 770-808-1955

ITEM	AMOUNT
Subtotal	
Postage & Handling (Call for Shipping Charges)	
C.O.D. (Add $6 plus Postage & Handling)	
Total	

Name _____ Date _____

Address_____Apt./Unit_____

City_____ State_____ Zip_____

Credit Card Type: ☐ VISA   ☐ MasterCard   ☐ AMEX

Credit Card #_____ Exp. _____

Visit our website @ www.ormanpress.com
Your one-stop store for Christian resources!

Pastor and Sister McCalep are available to conduct
workshops and seminars on all of these resources.
Call 404-486-6740 for scheduling information.